Teaching in a World of Change

THE PROFESSIONAL EDUCATION FOR TEACHERS SERIES

Under the Editorship of PAUL WOODRING

Editor of the Educational Supplement of the Saturday Review
and Distinguished Service Professor at Western Washington State College

PUBLISHED TITLES

Introduction to American Education, Paul Woodring

Education and Democratic Ideals, Gordon C. Lee

Education in Western Culture, Robert Ulich

American Secondary Schools, Mauritz Johnson, Jr.

Teaching in a World of Change, Robert H. Anderson

Measuring Pupil Achievement and Aptitude, C. M. Lindvall

Volumes on the following topics are in preparation: Elementary Education, Human Growth and Development, Learning in the Schools, Social Psychology in Education.

Teaching in

a World of Change

ROBERT H. ANDERSON
Harvard University

Harcourt, Brace & World, Inc.
New York · Chicago · Burlingame

Library of Congress Catalog Card Number: 66–25135

Printed in the United States of America

Editor's Foreword

The history of innovation in American education, as Professor Anderson makes clear in this volume, is not a happy one. For a variety of reasons, not the least of which has been the resistance of teachers to change, many sound ideas for improvements in the schools have been rejected without adequate trial. At best, under our decentralized system, change comes at different rates in different schools. Some schools have scarcely begun to adapt their programs to the new demands and the new opportunities of the second half of the twentieth century. But it is now clear that, as a nation, we have entered into a period of dramatic educational reform that will bring substantial changes to all levels of education, from the nursery school through the university. And, in a time of change, it is essential that programs of teacher education prepare teachers for the schools of the future rather than for those of the past.

The student now in college is likely to find, when he becomes a teacher, that both the school and the teacher's role have changed substantially during the few years that have elapsed since the day when he was himself a pupil. In all probability he received his own elementary education in a series of self-contained classrooms, each called a "grade," and his high-school education through a series of courses or subjects each taught by a different teacher whose work was largely independent of the work of other teachers. In each of his classes there were about thirty pupils regardless of the subject of instruction or the type of activity in which the pupils engaged. He has some understanding of the role of the teacher in such a school and looks forward to such a role for himself.

But when he returns to teach in one of these schools it is entirely possible that he may become a member of a teaching team or find himself in a school in which pupils are not assigned to grades. Instead of teaching uniform classes of thirty boys and girls, he may be expected to work with much smaller groups for some part of the day and with larger groups at other times. He will almost certainly discover that both the content and the organization of the curriculum have changed. He will be expected to use new educational technology and to adapt his teaching to programed instruction. And he will find that these changes make it necessary for the teacher to play a new and different role.

This book will help future teachers prepare themselves for that new role by making them better aware of the changes they will face, of the forces behind those changes, and of the opportunities those changes offer. It will help each teacher evaluate the proposed innovations and adapt them to the special characteristics of his own pupils. It will help him decide which innovations to accept and which to reject.

Like the other volumes in this series, this book can be used in a variety of ways, depending on the organization of the courses prescribed. Supplemented by the readings listed at the end of each chapter, it can provide the basis for a new course. Some instructors may wish to use it as one of the textbooks in a comprehensive course in educational principles, methodology, and school organization. Still others may use it in connection with a seminar that accompanies practice teaching or internship. And older teachers will find it excellent as a means of bringing themselves up to date on new approaches to education.

Professor Anderson is exceptionally well qualified to describe the innovations in American education, recount their history, evaluate their promise, and place them in their proper perspective as a part of the educational revolution of the 1960's. As a professor in the Harvard Graduate School of Education and as a director of research programs, he has played a distinguished role in the educational improvements of recent years. He has worked closely with public school teachers engaged in experimentation. His many publications, particularly those on the organization of nongraded schools, are well known to professional educators. With the publication of this volume his views and interpretations, as well as his broad knowledge of the empirical evidence from research, become available in convenient form to the teachers of tomorrow.

PAUL WOODRING

Preface

When this volume was first proposed for the Professional Education for Teachers Series, it carried the tentative title "Innovation and Change in American Education." While it was in preparation, however, its emphasis shifted from a general survey of current innovations to a reexamination of the context within which the modern American teacher works. What finally came of my labors (no book, I have found, is ever really "finished") is primarily aimed at informing and influencing those who work or are planning to work with children.

The three-sided view of teaching presented in the first two chapters serves as a premise on which all the other proposals and ideas are based. The remaining chapters explore and elaborate various questions of school organization and grouping, roles within the school, school architecture, and the school library's functions. All these discussions are intended to reveal ways in which the schools themselves are changing, or can be changed, for the better and ways in which the role of the teacher is becoming more challenging and interesting.

There are three major topics that I have deliberately neglected, partly because of my limitations and partly because other writers have already provided an excellent frame of reference. For example, John I. Goodlad's summary of the curriculum reforms under way in the United States [1] discusses how "things to be learned" are changing. Excellent clues to the ways in which "pedagogy" is maturing as a field of study are to be found in the writings of Jerome Bruner (especially his latest work, *Toward a Theory of Instruction* [2]) and in *Theories of Learning and Instruction* (the 1964 Yearbook of the National Society for the Study of Education). Emerging instructional resources—the third topic that I have more or less neglected—are

1. *School Curriculum Reform in the United States,* New York: Fund for the Advancement of Education, 1964.
2. Cambridge, Mass.: Harvard University Press, 1966.

only briefly covered (in chapter eight, in particular), but a great deal of other material is available on computers and self-instructional devices, communications media, and other technical resources. I have chosen to concentrate on those topics that are within my experience and on which more emphasis and clarification seem to be needed.

Several authorities have rightly commented that the impact and potency of such arrangements as nongrading and cooperative teaching, despite their high potential, have been to date disappointingly low. In chapters four and five, however, it is hoped that the reader will discover or confirm reasons for supporting these arrangements. It is hoped, too, that chapters six, seven, and eight will inspire him to work in his own community for better school buildings, better library facilities, and personnel arrangements that will raise teaching to the status it deserves.

Many have contributed to both the ideology and the format of this volume. With respect to ideas in particular I shall always be indebted to John Goodlad and Glen Heathers, in whose friendship I constantly rejoice and from whom I have learned much more than I have given. Too many to mention are my colleagues in Lexington, in Newton, and in the Harvard-Lexington Summer Program (later renamed the Harvard-Boston Program) from whom I borrowed copiously while developing a frame of reference for teaching. No one was more generous with time and suggestions than Henry F. Olds, Jr., and valuable help was also given by Walter Hill and Cynthia Ritsher. The important contribution of Sara Jaffarian is evident in chapter eight.

By coincidence, I completed the final manuscript for this book almost exactly twenty-five years from the date I first became a salaried teacher in Oconomowoc, Wisconsin. I find myself wondering how the young teacher named Anderson, now so profoundly changed by a quarter-century of experience and study, would then have reacted to the ideas he has placed between these covers. Even more intriguing is the question of how far the literature of 1991, written by the generation now serving as apprentices, will have gone beyond our own primitive conception of teaching!

Since this book is for and about teachers, it seems especially fitting to dedicate it to those who taught me. In particular, I would like to salute Ralph W. Tyler, for his continuing leadership at the top of American education, and to pay tribute to the memory of Virgil E. Herrick and William Claude Reavis.

ROBERT H. ANDERSON

Contents

Teaching in a World of Change

Chapter One

Innovation and Change
as a Characteristic of the Times

The young adult preparing to enter the teaching profession in the late 1960's, whether as upperclassman or as graduate student, encounters problems and opportunities quite different from those his predecessors faced. The demands made by a rapidly changing and increasingly complex society have radically altered the teacher's role and the conditions under which that role is carried out. The prospective teacher finds that the concept of teaching he formed as a student, and sometimes even the concept of teaching that informs his professional training, is either obsolescent or obsolete. The ways in which the teacher's role is changing and the forces that are reshaping programs and procedures in the schools are matters of compelling importance to the teacher-to-be.

Our specific objective in this book is to examine the forces and events that have led to one of the most active and promising periods of educational reform in history and to examine the current status and future prospects of some of the ideas and mechanisms on which that reform is based. These ideas and mechanisms are not really as new as the term "innovation" implies. Most of them can be traced back through decades and even centuries of professional enterprise. Yet many of them took on their current shape and significance in the mid-1950's. Sometime between 1955 and 1960, give or take a few years, they went through several stages of design, exploratory implementation, redesign, and general dissemination. Both the speed and the earnestness with which these ideas were developed have had a dramatic effect on the climate of professional education.

Many of these developments took place in the secondary schools, some in the colleges. Consequently, at least a few of the future teachers now in preprofessional course work have participated as students in some of the pilot projects. Nevertheless, it will be many years before any significant number of future teachers will have

3

had as children any substantial experience with the ideas we will be discussing in this book. Furthermore, it will be several years before large numbers of newly trained teachers will be employed in schools where these ideas are in routine and successful use. Still, innovation-minded new teachers will find increasing opportunities to take part as pioneers in initiating such programs or in improv-- ing those that have already been launched. And the possibility of their being employed in a school that deliberately avoids or dis- avows innovative programs may virtually disappear within another decade or two.

This is not to say that the procedures and practices discussed in this book have already proved themselves or have assumed their ultimate form. There is an almost desperate need for patience and intelligence in examining their potential merit and in putting them to a proper test. Even though the climate of the 1960's is remarkably hospitable to basic educational reform, there is a danger that some potentially good ideas and practices will be damaged by careless handling and premature evaluation.

Over the past century or so, many innovations in education have met that fate. Although some of them have had a lasting influence and have reappeared in somewhat modified form, most of them have fizzled out. Some were essentially poor ideas, and so deserved their fate. Others were excellent ideas, but they were mishandled or distorted in the process of implementation. A few good ideas failed simply because they were introduced at an inappropriate time or because the entrenched educational establishment set up insur- mountable resistance and obstruction to them. Others were on the verge of succeeding, but their proponents were not sufficiently skilled in research or flexible enough in their expectations to rec- ognize and follow up what they had accomplished. In summary, then, the history of experimentation in American public education has for the most part been a story of failure. Such progress as has been made has taken place only at a glacial rate.

Never in the past has there been a situation quite like that in the United States in the 1960's. Educational reform now seems to be a recognized need in all segments of society. Our population cycle and our manpower requirements have combined in such a way as to make the well-trained teacher both a statistical rarity and a factor in national defense. The intense competition for able college graduates, aggravated by a postwar population boom that filled the nation's classrooms, focused national attention on teacher recruitment. Ways of relieving the teacher shortage, such as the use of nonprofessional assistants, and ways of widening the influence of superior teachers, such as the use of educational television, came under serious consideration. The nation's preoccupation with Russian competition, spurred by Sputnik and the cosmonauts, led to vigorous support of reforms in science, mathematics, foreign languages, and technical education. The national talent hunt led to great public concern for gifted children and their oft-wasted capacities, and the long overdue recognition of socioeconomic injustices led, much more recently, to a national realization of the great inequities that exist in the educational opportunities of white versus Negro, rich versus poor, urban versus suburban, and culturally privileged versus culturally disadvantaged.

There are other explanations for the apparent willingness of the average American taxpayer to contemplate basic changes in his community's schools. He is himself a creature of a changing world, and he is quite aware that his children will need more and better education to survive. He realizes that the education that was sufficient to his father's needs, and even to his own needs, cannot prepare his children for the world of the future. He appreciates, more keenly with each passing year, what the eminent anthropologist, Margaret Mead, said in 1951:

> American children are growing up within the most rapidly changing culture of which we have any record in the world, within a culture where for several generations each generation's experience has differed sharply from the last, and in which the experience of the youngest child in a large family will be extraordinarily different from that of the first born. Mothers cannot look back to the experience of their mothers, nor even to that of their older sisters; young husbands and fathers have no guides to the behavior which they are assuming today. So long standing and so rapid have been those processes of change that expectation of change and anxiety about change have been built into our character as a people.[1]

He has seen automation become a reality; his own job has probably become more technical; he is aware of computers and data-processing machines; and he knows that new tools of research and development are helping man to acquire new knowledge and to discard false ideas at a truly prodigious rate. In one brief lifetime, he has seen the transformation of industrial practices, scientific

---

1. Margaret Mead, "The Impact of Culture on Personality Development in the United States Today," *Understanding the Child*, 20 (January 1951), pp. 17–18.

and medical research, and even social research from a stage of moderate efficiency to one of almost miraculous speed and accomplishment. With such experiences to guide him, little wonder that he begins to ask questions about the school's efficiency and modernity!

Oddly enough, though, the average citizen is more likely to understate than to overstate the need for modernizing the schools, for he has long been accustomed to the soothing reassurances of professional educators that "all is well" in the classrooms. All too seldom has the school administrator given his patrons an objective report of the school's problems, needs, and shortcomings; his tendency has been, rather, to emphasize the positive and to take comfort in those accomplishments (such as "acceptable" scores on standardized tests) that favorably link the local effort to national norms. All too seldom has a school administrator or a teaching staff taken a strong and militant stand against overcrowded classrooms, shortages of instructional resources, the curtailment of services, or other manifestations of educational neglect. All too rarely, in fact, have national professional organizations and even university professors cried out against the "creeping mediocrity" of American schools in general or against specific conditions injurious to child welfare and learning. Although many school people have worried about these problems, it has been only since about 1955, when Rudolf Flesch opened Pandora's box with his abrasive *Why Johnny Can't Read,* that there has been any considerable public discussion *by educators* of the real weaknesses in the schools. The layman, therefore, has had in recent years an eye-opening and sobering introduction to the real problems that beset the schools.

For the educator too the past decade has been a time of mixed frustration and excitement. He too has seen the world changing around him. He has seen his personal life and habits radically affected by medical, social, economic, industrial, political, and cultural developments. He has seen what the computer can do to increase the administrative efficiency of his schools; he has found himself collaborating with university scholars on pilot programs in curriculum development; he has been inundated with books and articles describing this panacea and that; he has heard rumors that teaching machines and other devices will take over his work; and he has felt the sting of criticism for his time-honored habits of professional isolationism and adherence to grade-level–expectancy standards. At the same time, he has watched with apprehension as various groups have captured the national spotlight by attacking progressivism in the schools, or by electing reactionary school-board members and administrative officials, or by advocating a return to the McGuffey readers, or by cracking down on rising school costs by eliminating some of the practices and programs that are most desperately needed if the schools are to deal effectively with the changing world. Alternately enchanted by the bright possibilities inherent in pilot projects of research and development and overwhelmed by the magnitude of the problems and obstacles with which he is confronted, the educator finds it difficult to define his own role and to decide upon a course of action.

This book springs from several premises about the current state of public education and about the conditions that must be satisfied if the schools are to succeed:

1. Although the United States may take justifiable pride in the accomplishments of its decentralized school system, the first in the world to provide significant educational opportunity for virtually every citizen, it must look with great concern at the gap between *what could be* (given present knowledge) and *what is* in the schools.

2. Our society promises to change in the future, perhaps even more rapidly and fundamentally than it has in the recent past. The gap between an attainable ideal and the actual situation, then, is likely to widen with each passing day unless the schools find ways to adjust to or direct some of the forces that are creating change.

3. The things that children may need to learn with the help of the schools are multiplying at an overwhelming rate, and this rate promises to increase. Conversely, many things that were once thought to be true and a necessary part of school learning are being discarded or modified at a very rapid rate. It is therefore urgently necessary to assemble the profession, both nationally and locally, for continuous and intensive reexamination of the curriculum and its objectives.

4. The rate at which knowledge is expanding makes it increasingly unlikely that any one teacher can have a sufficient command of the overall curriculum, as in the so-called self-contained elementary-school classroom, or even of a single content field, as in the secondary-school department, to function independently. The inevitable result of the expansion of knowledge must be a recourse to faculty specialization in some form or another.

5. Like society in general, education is currently experiencing

an almost explosive development of new technologies. The relevance and potential of the new tools and arrangements called forth by experimentation must be examined with great care, and those judged meritorious must be placed in general service more rapidly than new technologies have been in the past.

6. For countless years the teaching profession has made pious pronouncements about individual differences, about the unique value and merit of each individual, and about providing for the needs and welfare of each child. Recent research has revealed how truly great are the differences among and within individuals and has uncovered startling evidence of the great variety of ways in which people can and do learn. It has also confirmed what critics have long suspected: that the school has had little success in providing for each unique individual's needs.

7. Although it has become almost automatic to refer to teaching as a profession, teachers only rarely possess the specialized knowledge and resources that should distinguish them from other well-educated but nonteaching persons. Teachers perform many tasks that could be performed as well by high-school students; they sometimes have only token training for their teaching role; they rarely assert their autonomy either individually or collectively; and they do not always have the single-minded and dedicated attitude toward their work that is characteristic of doctors, lawyers, ministers, and engineers. Although in this book the word *profession* will frequently be used in reference to teaching and teachers, the term is used primarily as a convenience and in part to reflect the author's strong hopes that it may soon be deserved.

8. Three words that are used with increasing frequency in discussions of educational improvement are *excellence, flexibility,* and *efficiency.* Excellence is what we want each child, no matter how different he is from all others, to reach—that state of physical health and intellectual-psychological maturity of which he is potentially capable. Flexibility means having and exploiting a number of alternatives in the use of personnel, facilities, and resources, and in responding to the needs and interests of children. Efficiency is the performance of carefully defined tasks at the lowest possible cost in time, money, and energy. It is the author's conviction that some of the practices described in this book are capable of increasing the flexibility and the efficiency of the schools and, therefore, of contributing to the ideal of bringing each unique child to the peak of his God-given power.

Suggestions for Further Reading

A general introduction to the scope and the many dimensions of the current unrest in education may be obtained by a brief examination of the following books: Ronald Gross and Judith Murphy, eds., *The Revolution in the Schools*, New York: Harcourt, Brace, & World, 1964; Alfred de Grazia and David A. Sohn, eds., *Revolution in Teaching: New Theory, Technology, and Curricula*, New York: Bantam, 1964; John I. Goodlad, ed., *The Changing American School*, The Sixty-fifth Yearbook of the National Society for the Study of Education, Part II, Chicago: Univ. of Chicago Press, 1966.

Chapter Two

Teaching as a Career

Not so very long ago in the United States the medical doctor was by no means as competent and respected as he is today. At the turn of the century medical schools were poorly staffed, and the men who practiced medicine were often poorly educated, poorly grounded in science, and ill equipped to handle the complex problems that came up every day. For many centuries, in fact, people literally feared for their lives when they subjected themselves to the care of a physician.

To the current generation of young Americans, the beneficiaries of the best medical care the world has ever known, this fact of history must seem very strange indeed. Though physicians remain human and subject to occasional tragic error, their remarkable knowledge and skill have earned for them a position of great prestige in our society. Medical schools and research hospitals are among the nation's most prized resources, and few Americans begrudge physicians and surgeons the generally comfortable standard of living their income permits. To the ambitious young college student, medicine usually appears as a very attractive career, albeit a most arduous and demanding one. To the man on the street, Dr. Kildare or Dr. Casey presents an awe-inspiring and positive image, and only rarely is the doctor portrayed in movies or novels in an uncomplimentary light. "It is a good thing to be a doctor."

It is probably fair to say that lawyers, too, enjoy relatively high prestige in our culture. The public is aware of the rigorous requirements in most states for legal training and admission to the bar and appreciates the competitive and intellectually demanding nature of legal work.

If we were to ask the man on the street, in any town in America, what he would like his son or his grandson to choose as a vocation, he would probably mention medicine, or law, or some profession other than teaching. The teacher has never enjoyed great prestige or high salary in this country, and the typical feeling toward teachers has rarely been one of admiration. Gratitude, perhaps, but not admiration.

Americans tend to regard teaching as a relatively pleasant and comfortable life, even though they realize that teachers must shoulder certain occasionally distasteful responsibilities for dealing with the rambunctious young! It is a role to which one can aspire even though one has limited means, since it requires considerably fewer years of university training than do medicine and law. It offers, at least apparently, a more convenient and tolerable working calendar, with frequent and lengthy vacations and the possibility of travel or interesting summer employment as an escape from monotony. To the man on the street, who probably enjoys the company of his own children, teaching may even seem a pleasant social experience with friendly students and cheerful colleagues all enjoying the modern architecture and controlled climate of a well-designed building.

Success in teaching, it is widely believed, comes to those who (1) have completed a college education and therefore possess knowledge to be dispensed, (2) are sufficiently firm and dignified to be able to maintain discipline and hold the respect of their pupils, (3) have sufficient administrative talents to ensure good record keeping and property accounting, and (4) are exemplary adults, offering an attractive but conventional model to the young in their charge.

This is scarcely an acceptable description of the professional teacher. It is a stereotype—one that has in recent years been giving way to a more realistic estimate. However, the sad fact is that the role of the American teacher has been awkwardly and imperfectly defined even by teachers themselves, and the uncomplimentary stereotype is one that the profession must outlive even as did medicine in this century.

One of the unpleasant truths we must face is that the typical American teacher, along with many administrators and supervisors, is not very well prepared. Our man on the street, if he is a college graduate, probably is only slightly less qualified to teach than is a college graduate with a teacher's certificate. Since standards of certification are low, and since the caliber of professional education courses ranges all the way from excellent to poor, the certified teacher is not always the fully qualified professional that we assume he is. Many thousands of teachers still in service were admitted under even less demanding certification regulations than those in effect today, and their only real qualification for the role is represented in their loyalty to children and in whatever valid translations they have been able to make of their experiences in the classroom.

Deficiencies in the preservice preparation of teachers tend to persist throughout their years in service. Although some teachers complete worthwhile master's degree programs, most teachers undertake little formal or informal professional training once they have settled into the teaching role. The old cliché about "twenty years' experience" being "the same experience twenty times over" may be an overstatement, but it does have a grain of truth. Teachers tend to stay with the routines they establish in their first few years of teaching; they receive very little information or helpful criticism from their colleagues and superiors; and they derive little benefit from the various "in-service education" programs sponsored from time to time (if at all) by the school authorities.

Elementary-school teachers, in particular, seem to develop routines that leave little time for reflection, meditation, analysis, and long-range professional planning. True, their daily schedules are usually crammed with a host of duties, and they have somewhat less unscheduled time than do secondary-school teachers. However, studies of how elementary-school teachers use their time reveal that even under favorable conditions they spend only trivial amounts of time on nonroutine matters. Studies of their reading habits, for example, show that they seldom subscribe to (or regularly read) professional journals in their field, much less scholarly journals in general, and that they have at best a superficial acquaintance with the more prominent and provocative books that are published in elementary education. Of course, many journal articles and textbooks in elementary education scarcely deserve serious readership; yet the failure to consult the *best* available publications does seem to betray an unprofessional or even a nonintellectual mindset.

The record of secondary-school teachers is slightly better, perhaps because they tend to have a greater commitment to a particular field with a literature of its own. The teacher of social studies, for example, has access to several journals in social-studies education and to countless publications in history, geography, economics, political science, and so on. Reading habits established in undergraduate or graduate school are likely to persist, at least in the young teacher, and books by distinguished historians, economists, or other scholars are therefore likely to come to the teacher's attention. Moreover, in a high school there is likely to be a group of teachers with whom the teacher can discuss the newest book on John F. Kennedy, or the pre-Columbian "Vinland Map," or someone's new approach to the social studies.

However, the secondary-school teacher is only *less* negligent than the elementary-school teacher in such matters as reading, reflecting, and planning; he is usually not enjoying a vigorous intellectual life. More often than not he even neglects his scholarship. A recent study of several hundred history teachers in public high schools, conducted at Indiana University,[1] found that the great majority read virtually nothing in their field from year to year and that many of them did not even know the names of prominent present-day historians. Other studies show that high-school teachers also neglect their pedagogical scholarship; they are too enmeshed in trivial activities to sit back and meditate over the tone and quality of their teaching. They too have at best a superficial acquaintance with the more provocative writings in education and are betrayed by a phlegmatic attitude toward the raw and unsolved problems of their calling.

CRITICISM: THE MISSING INGREDIENT

The American teacher typically lives and dies without having experienced any professional criticism except in small, economy-sized doses. (By using the adjective "professional" we intend to exclude that form of criticism, sometimes unwarranted and sometimes not, meted out by parents. Most teachers, however, suffer relatively little severe criticism even from parents.) One of the most common complaints voiced by student teachers is that their professors and master teachers tend to withhold criticism and offer only positive encouragement and reassurance. And when they take on their first jobs as fledgling teachers, they are surprised to find that the principal tends to "let them alone" and pays little attention to their performance. Even the experienced teachers in the school, though they are usually friendly and helpful when approached, seem reluctant to intervene in the young teacher's work

---

1. See Maurice G. Baxter, Robert H. Ferrell, and John E. Wiltz, *The Teaching of American History in High Schools,* Bloomington: Indiana Univ. Press, 1964, p. 160.

and assume that the youngster is wholly capable of performing the entire range of duties for which they themselves are also responsible. Some first-year teachers find this lack of interest on the part of supervisors and colleagues disappointing and even disillusioning.

Actually, the professional growth and even the professional survival of the American teacher depend on his exposure to objective and informed criticism: criticism of his goals and of the relationship of his activities to those goals; criticism of his teaching style, of his relationship to children, of the entire pattern of his teaching maneuvers; and criticism of his procedures and conclusions in evaluation. Teachers go through life talking (and gossiping) together about many, many things, but only rarely do they examine teaching by analyzing their own personal experiences. There is, in short, almost no personally meaningful dialogue about teaching among the colleagues in a school.

The reasons for this situation are not hard to find. For one thing, teaching is a rather vaguely defined role, and standards of excellence are not well established. Most supervisors are not particularly well trained in either pedagogy or supervision, and they tend to be more concerned with maintaining a friendly, happy social atmosphere in the school than with the tough-minded business of evaluating and improving the intellectual environment. For years the literature of school administration and supervision has emphasized "democratic leadership" (or words to the same effect). Often, however, this worthy concept has been distorted into a kind of spineless, don't-let-me-get-in-your-way, I'm-just-one-of-the-boys attitude. Teachers, too, sometimes overvalue their privacy, perhaps because they realize that much of what they are doing would not bear close inspection. For these and other reasons, supervision has usually ended in a kind of stalemate, and the tasks of the teacher have enjoyed very little analysis in depth.

DIMENSIONS OF THE TEACHER'S WORK

What, then, is teaching? What do we mean when we refer to a person as a teacher? A discussion of these questions will be useful later on when we consider how some of the new patterns of school organization seek to redefine the teacher's responsibilities and influence the ways in which his talents are used.

What follows is doubtless an oversimplification, but it is merely an effort to describe some of the dimensions of the teacher's life and role. It does not spell out what the teacher actually does, but it tries to suggest how his varied activities are related to one another.

Everyone in a vocational role develops an ideal image of that role and an image of himself as a practitioner of that role. He also develops a set of satisfactions and dissatisfactions that stem from his acceptance or nonacceptance of both the ideal image and his own. Obviously his morale and, yes, his success in the role will be very directly related to the satisfactions that he does or does not feel, and the actual value of his services to his employer or the consumer may depend on how closely his definition of the role resembles the "true" definition.

To try to offer a "true definition" of teaching might seem presumptuous. To propose one way of looking at the teacher's life and the satisfactions and obligations that attach to his work may be helpful.

Relationships to Learners. First of all, in order to be a teacher one must have pupils, and one must be capable of negotiating satisfactory relationships with them. In the hearts and minds of many teachers, one of the most important and satisfying things about teaching is the personal, sometimes affectionate relationship that grows between the teacher and the attractive young human beings who are his pupils. Ordinarily this is a legitimate, wholesome satisfaction in teaching, just as it is in nursing, medicine, social work, and other service professions. Furthermore, many children are in need of a pleasant relationship with an adult, and a friendly response from the teacher may contribute significantly to a child's personal development.

Sometimes, however, teachers carry this personal relationship too far. Especially in the elementary school, teachers occasionally seek to develop a very deep rapport with children and make demands on them for personal response. Teachers with a neurotic disability or an excessive dependence on children for the gratification of their own emotional needs can do considerable damage. Fortunately, such teachers are in a distinct minority. But there is a much larger number who, though not emotionally disabled or improperly motivated, overemphasize personal relationships.

In most circumstances, the appropriate relationship between the teacher and the learner is essentially objective and "on the friendly side of neutral." The teacher should of course be friendly and should reveal a sincere interest in the well-being of his pupils. He should, however, be businesslike rather than chummy, appreciative rather than assuasive and tender. The effect of his behavior should be to assure the child of his positive interest in the child's personal and educational growth, to convince the child that he possesses knowledge and talents that the child can use, and to persuade the child that he is earnest and well-meaning in the program he has planned.

In short, the effect of the teacher' behavior should be to elicit the child's trust in the teacher's motives, in his competency, and in the relevance of his work to the child's own interests. The child who has trust in his teacher is miles ahead of the child who has not!

The nature of the tasks will depend in part on the teacher's skill as a clinical observer of each pupil and as a diagnostician of each pupil's needs. He is, in a sense, a "student of learners"—a professional scholar of children. He must have a fund of general information about how children grow, about how they learn, and about the things that children of a particular age group customarily do, think, and feel. In addition, he must learn as much as he can about the specific youngsters with whom he deals, both as a group and as individuals. This *diagnostic* relationship to the child, which resembles that of a physician to a young patient, serves as the principal basis for the teacher's educational planning and decisions.

Relationships to the Content of the School Program. The teacher has certain knowledge, skills, insights, and attitudes and it is his responsibility to pass these on to the pupils in his charge—either in a didactic fashion or in some more indirect or subtle way. For simplicity let us use the word "knowledge" to represent all the facts, tools, concepts, ideas, and other "things to be taught." What should be the teacher's relationship to this knowledge? The answer may seem obvious, but it is an essential part of our definition of teaching.

Clearly the teacher must have a *command* of the knowledge he is to teach. Since factual knowledge is growing so rapidly, this is an increasingly difficult feat. Hence, the teacher must be an active scholar of his field or fields. In particular, he must have control of the so-called process goals that enable students to acquire, interpret, evaluate, and communicate knowledge: (1) tool skills, (2) critical thinking, (3) creative thinking, (4) inquiry, (5) self-instruction, (6) self-evaluation, (7) interests, and (8) study habits.[2]

In addition, the teacher must have a special *commitment* to the knowledge he is to teach. This is more an emotional than an intellectual commitment, since we are referring to the feeling the teacher has for his subject and to his conviction that the subject matter is important for the learner to possess.

Command and commitment, then, are the two kinds of relationship that a truly professional teacher seeks to have to the content of the school program for which he is responsible.

Pedagogy: The Basis of a Professional Status. The third ingredient of the teacher's work is pedagogy, the art and science of instruction, the use of certain methods and strategies to bring about learning in the pupil. Pedagogy is the discipline that examines what the teacher does to inform, to stimulate, to activate the learner in ways that build a bridge between the learner and what he is to learn. In one sense teaching is an art, because it calls for inventiveness, ingenuity, and originality in response to unexpected or unpredictable situations. It is also a science, because it derives from an increasingly precise understanding of how children learn and of the predictable effects of certain procedures and technologies that the profession has developed and tested. The art-science of instructing, then, adds what we may call the pedagogical dimension to teaching.

The need for a more highly developed technology of teaching is urgent. As we discover more about the many different ways in which children actually learn, we realize that we must have a greater range of consciously selected alternatives in methodology. As other projects demonstrate the powers and also the limits of new devices and approaches, the basis for an intelligent selection of one or the other alternative becomes clearer. As teachers are brought into more intimate professional contact, and as their conversation focuses more analytically upon the strategies and tools that are in use, an awareness grows of the need for more careful and precise planning and for more relevant and appropriate ways of presenting ideas and materials to the children.

Many teachers have only a limited and inadequate repertoire of

2. See Glen Heathers, "Team Teaching and the Educational Reform Movement," *Team Teaching,* Judson T. Shaplin and Henry F. Olds, Jr., eds., New York: Harper and Row, 1964, pp. 345–75.

teaching skills. They reveal their poor command of pedagogical principles and of technical and strategic resources in many ways: by the manner in which they introduce new materials, by the types of question and feedback mechanism they use, by their tendency to talk and inform rather than to listen and guide, by their exclusive dependence on the procedures suggested in textbooks and teacher's manuals, and by their heavy reliance on their own personality in holding pupil attention. Teaching in America is therefore highly idiosyncratic in some respects and yet quite standardized in its adherence to the procedures suggested in popular textbooks. Furthermore, a great deal of what takes place in American classrooms proves on close inspection to be unsuitable or even indefensible. Teachers should have a greater interest in examining their pedagogical behavior and in analyzing their instructional problems.

THE TEACHER'S ROLE: A SUMMARY

We have defined the teacher's role as having three major dimensions: (1) relationships to learners, (2) relationships to the content of the school program, and (3) depth in understanding of how learning takes place and of the art-science of instruction (pedagogy). The figure shows how the three dimensions of the teacher's role are related to one another. Note that we have chosen the shape of a right triangle. The base of the triangle depicts the teacher's relationships to children. The diagnostic function is represented by an arrow directed toward the learner, since this is a unilateral relationship. The interaction line is of course a two-way arrow.

The vertical side of the triangle represents the teacher's command of and commitment to the substance of teaching. The hypotenuse represents the pedagogical dimension, with an upward-directed arrow suggesting that the learner accepts (or reaches out for) the things that are to be learned and a downward-directed arrow representing the strategies and procedures the teacher uses to activate the reaching-out process.

It would be interesting to show this diagram to a large sample of American teachers and to ask them which side of the triangle represents, to them, the most satisfying dimension of teaching. How would you respond? Remember that a true definition of the teacher's role must include all three sides of the triangle. And yet, until very recently, many teachers have overemphasized either the importance of their relationships with children or their interest in the curriculum content and have underemphasized the pedagogical dimension on which their ultimate professional success depends.

According to Pythagoras' famous theorem, the square of the hypotenuse of a right triangle is equal to the sum of the squares of the other two sides. We can paraphrase this theorem and say: a command of pedagogy (artistry and proficiency in the instructional realm) is as important to the teacher's success and satisfaction as is the sum of his relationships to children and to knowledge!

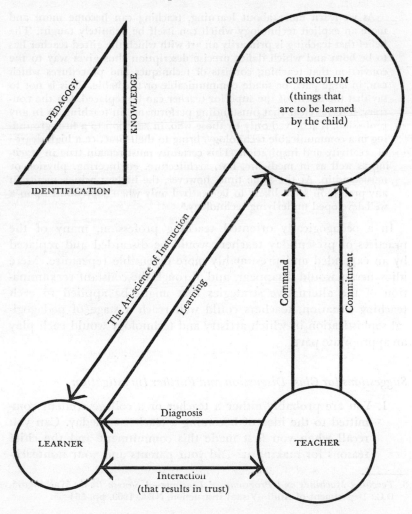

In short, we can say that the teacher of tomorrow, like the physician and surgeon of today, will achieve his professional reputation and derive his personal satisfaction primarily because of his technological and procedural proficiency. We do not deny that he must also have great skill in and may legitimately derive great pleasure from interaction with the children in his classes. Nor do we deny that the same must be true with respect to the substance of his teaching. All we are emphasizing here is the great significance that must be accorded to pedagogy in particular.

As A. A. Lumsdaine and Robert Glaser have said:

> As we learn more about learning, teaching can become more and more an explicit technology which can itself be definitely taught. The belief that teaching is primarily an art with which the gifted teacher has to be born and which defies precise description thus gives way to the conviction that teaching consists of techniques and procedures which can, in large part, be made communicable or teachable. This is not to say that the talent of the superior teacher can be replaced. On the contrary, it seems clear that outstanding performance in teaching, as in any profession, is achieved only by those who, in addition to a firm grounding in a communicable technology, bring to their practice a high degree of creativity and inspiration. This certainty must remain true in teaching as well as in medicine, law, architecture, engineering, physics, or musicianship. At the same time, however, the highest achievements in any profession seem likely to be realized only when they build upon a well-developed underlying technology.[3]

In a pedagogically oriented teaching profession, many of the practices of present-day teachers would be discarded and replaced by an expanded and presumably more defensible repertoire. Mere idiosyncrasy would disappear, and, through the constant reexamination of the alternative strategies that might be applied to each teaching situation, teachers could well reach a stage of pedagogical sophistication in which artistry and technology would each play an appropriate part.

Suggestions for Class Discussion and Further Investigation

1. You are probably either a teacher or a college student committed to the idea of becoming a teacher someday. Can you recall when you first made this commitment and the chief reasons for making it? Did your parents and your nonteach-

---

3. *Teaching Machines and Programmed Learning—A Source Book*, Washington, D.C.: Department of Audio-Visual Instruction, NEA, 1960, pp. 564–65.

ing friends support your decision and for reasons compatible with your own? What difficulties or disappointments did you envisage?

2. Do you agree that criticism is an important but missing ingredient in the typical teacher's life? How eager are you to receive comments and reactions from other professional workers? Do you think your attitude is shared by others?

3. How well does the figure on page 19 describe the dimensions of teaching? Do you think most teachers would agree that pedagogy is an important but neglected dimension? What can you do to strengthen your talents along all three dimensions, particularly the pedagogical?

Suggestions for Further Reading

A very comprehensive volume on teaching, N. L. Gage, ed., *Handbook of Research Teaching,* Chicago: Rand McNally, 1963, was published under the sponsorship of the American Educational Research Association and is highly recommended as a general source. Nine chapters deal with teaching various grade levels and subject areas (for example, research on teaching secondary-school mathematics).

In the *Elementary School Journal,* 66 (November 1965), pp. 63–67, you will find two thought-provoking articles by Ezra Wyeth and Benjamin D. Wright concerning the bad public image of teachers. In the December 1965 issue of the same magazine, Carol leFevre provides some sobering answers to the question, "Why Teach?" (pp. 121-25). Discussion of these several articles is recommended.

An attempt to show the ways in which instruction, teaching, and learning differ from one another is provided by Elliot W. Eisner in "Instruction, Teaching, and Learning: An Attempt at Differentiation," *The Elementary School Journal,* 65 (December 1964), pp. 115–19.

A recent and valuable statement is Gordon C. Lee's chapter, "The Changing Role of the Teacher," *The Changing American School,* The Sixty-fifth Yearbook of the National Society for the Study of Education, Part II, Chicago: Univ. of Chicago Press, 1966.

Chapter Three

The Organization of Schools:
A General Discussion

We can use the term *organization* in a great many ways when we discuss the schools of America. We can speak of the broad general structure of the school enterprise, including the network of public and private schools at all levels from preschool through the university. We can talk about the relationships of governmental agencies to the schools, especially as sources of financial support and control, at the national, state, and local levels. We can refer to the size and characteristics of local administrative units and to the trend toward the elimination of small inefficient rural school districts through consolidation into larger units. In discussing the schools of our great cities we are more likely to speak of the unwieldy bureaucracy and efforts to create autonomous subdistricts within the sprawling totality. Finally, we can discuss school organization in terms of the socioeconomic factors that are related to such variables as community size, program costs, and impact on community life.

UNIT ORGANIZATION

Public-school organization also has a longitudinal dimension. Few school districts are so small and compact that they can offer their entire range of services in a single setting under the same administration. Rather, they break up their program into a minimum of two or three separate units: the elementary school, sometimes a middle school or a junior high school, and a high school. The elementary school may or may not include a kindergarten for five-year-olds at the lower end, and it may include either the so-called sixth grade or the seventh and eighth grades at the upper end. The middle unit may embrace grades 7 and 8, or 7, 8, and 9, or, in a more recent trend, 6, 7, and 8. The high school, by the same token, may embrace either grades 9 through 12 or only 10 through 12. In smaller communities that are unable to support separate junior-high and senior-high units of efficient size, it is fairly common to find a six-year junior-senior high school embracing grades 7 through 12.

Although these are the most common patterns, an almost unlimited variety of patterns is possible. K8–4 (that is, kindergarten and the first eight grades in one unit and the four grades 9 through 12 in the other) was at one time the most prevalent pattern, but K6–6 and K6–3–3 or K6–2–4 had become prevalent by midcentury. The past decade has seen a rising interest in K4–4–4, with a "middle school" for grades 5 through 8. This pattern and the K5–3–4 pattern have been most prominent in states where legislation and arrangements for the financial support of the schools tend to favor the separation of grade 8 (historically the last year of the common, tax-supported school) and grade 9 (the freshman year of the secondary school, which later came to be part of the tax-supported common-school system).

Advocates of K5–3–4 or K4–4–4 also point out that when grade 9 is reattached to the senior high school, the remaining middle unit lacks flexibility and depth unless at least grade 6 is added to provide a three-year age span within the school. Experience with K6–2–4 and similar plans encompassing a two year age span in one of the units would seem to support the general principle that at least a three-year span is desirable under most circumstances.

The K4–4–4 and K5–3–4 patterns are recommended by some educators for one other important reason. They point out that the term *junior high* as associated with the K6–2–4 or K6–3–3 middle unit tended to endow it with various psychological and administrative characteristics better avoided in a school serving the early adolescent. Rather than becoming a legitimate and appropriate institution with its own special flavor, some believe, the junior high school was often merely a junior version of the high school. Hence, these educators have urged the use of such terms as "the middle school" [1] to endow the unit with a personality and meaning of its own.

The history of the elementary school and the secondary school has been marked by several inconclusive experiences with one or

---

1. An excellent general discussion of the middle school is contained in Judith Murphy, *The Middle School*, New York: Educational Facilities Laboratories, 1965.

another of the possible patterns. Educators have argued that child-
dren at one stage or another of growth are either more or less
suited for the environment of the upper or the lower unit. For
example, it is currently argued that sixth-graders (that is, eleven-
year-olds) in the late 1960's are physically, socially, psychologically, and intellectually more mature than their counterparts in
former years and that they should therefore be included in the
junior high school (or whatever the middle unit is called). Sometimes overlooked in such arguments is that the same tendency is
found in younger and older children as well and that it may be
as easy to modify the school environment as it is to relocate age
groups. Others argue that the continuity and integrity of the
school program are better protected when a particular age group
either is included (as in the argument supporting four-year senior
high schools) or is not included (as in the reluctance of some to
include fifth-graders, or even sixth-graders, in the middle unit).
Since secondary schools are usually better equipped than elementary schools with specialized facilities for science, foreign languages,
and physical education, some argue that upper-elementary children will have superior educational opportunities in the secondary
buildings. Still others argue for one or another arrangement on
grounds of a more logical or efficient use of supervisory personnel.

Despite the vigor with which these various arguments are advanced, research offers few dependable guides as to whether K6–6,
K6–3–3, K6–2–4, K4–4–4, or any of the other patterns is in fact
superior on educational or other valid grounds. There are no final
answers, nor is it likely that there ever will be. We may be persuaded that three-year units have more inherent flexibility, or that
it is easier to administer and supervise a four-year language program
in high school, or that ten- and eleven-year old children are better
served in a higher school unit, but such persuasion is less than
proof that we should commit ourselves permanently to a particular arrangement. Furthermore, the emergence of the "nongraded
school" (see chapter four) and various new patterns of staff utilization has made it obsolete to speak of sharp dividing lines between
one school unit and another or to consider a particular age
group as being inevitably better off when exposed to a certain
school atmosphere and learning opportunity.

What is likely to happen is that the various units of each school
district will overlap, each lower unit offering at least a portion of
the educational and social opportunities that are abundant in the

next higher unit. At the same time, each higher unit will continue to provide—for some of its pupils—some of the opportunities that are characteristic of the lower unit. The idea of a definite break in atmosphere and learning activities between one unit and another is intolerable in the current climate of education. Consequently, much of the historical argument about how each unit should be defined is irrelevant to present-day school planning.

What is *not* irrelevant, however, is the stark matter of the rising cost of school construction. Depending on how one chooses to read the evidence about overcrowding and the need for both new and replacement classrooms, the nation is at this moment somewhere between a hundred thousand and a quarter of a million classrooms (or their equivalent) short of needed capacity. Rare indeed is the community that is not faced with an urgent space shortage, and virtually nonexistent is the community in which both the quantity and the quality of instructional space are adequate by modern standards. For example, at least two hundred thousand elementary classrooms in present use are forty or more years old. Furthermore, if team teaching and related patterns of variable-sized pupil groupings become widely accepted, major architectural changes could well become necessary in 90 percent of existing schools that are in good condition. Buildings that are so obsolete in design and so poor in physical condition will have to be replaced in any event.

This problem is closely related to decisions that must be made within individual school districts. If, for example, the two-year junior high school is, for whatever reason, in need of either modernization or expansion or both, and if elementary schools in the same community are feeling a slight pinch, the city fathers might solve both problems by moving the sixth-grade classes into the new wings of the junior high school and changing it into a "middle school." The program and the atmosphere there must, of course, be appropriate for the eleven-year-olds. Or, both the four-year senior high school and the K–8 elementary school may be experiencing serious overcrowding. Then the community might build a three-year junior high school or middle school to siphon off ninth-graders from the high school and seventh- and eighth-graders from the elementary school. It is unlikely that there would be any educational, social, or administrative disadvantage in the new arrangement that could not be offset by good planning and articulation, especially if the three separate units (elementary, junior high or

middle school, and senior high) functioned in parallel and overlapping ways.

The middle school idea has recently gained many supporters in
larger cities suffering from racial imbalance in the schools. These
advocates feel that the middle school allows youngsters with differ-
ing neighborhood backgrounds to be brought together two years
earlier than is possible where the neighborhood school units include
grades 5 and 6. Such arguments offer yet another plausible justification for the K4–4–4 idea.

The K4–4–4 arrangement must not, however, be endowed with
advantages it does not in fact possess. Some educators argue that
ninth-graders are out of place socially or biologically in the middle
unit, or imply that colleges refuse to acknowledge academic work
completed in the junior-high unit, or otherwise try to justify what
high-school departments may prefer simply for their own convenience. Such arguments may backfire as conditions and needs change.
Educators should start to talk more earnestly about making the
internal environment of each school what it could be, under a
variety of conditions, and spend less time raising imaginary objections to particular alternatives.

Within the total K–12 organization, then, each school district
is really quite free to solve some of its construction and organization problems in terms of such considerations as economic cost, administrative practicality, or social policy. Apart from the improb-
able event of a purely capricious decision or a failure to take a
sufficiently long-range view of needs, communities following such
a procedure are unlikely to build themselves into an awkward situation. It must be remembered, however, that this argument has
as its very foundation the assumption that, once built, the schools
will respond to their pupils' actual needs and interests in flexible
and appropriate ways. None of the levels of school organization—
for young children, for the middle group, or for older adolescents—
has an automatic monopoly on these qualities.

THE SIZE OF SCHOOLS

How large should a school be? When is a school too small to be
efficient or too large to be comfortable? As we consider optimum
school organization, what can we confidently say about building
size that seems to be valid—at least in the present, primitive stage
of research on schools as physical entities?

First, as in the case of the division of school units within a district, decisions about optimum school size may be made on economic and other practical grounds as well as on theoretical grounds. Although sociological research may eventually yield some answers, we do not yet know whether small schools or large schools are better. What we *do* know is that schools need to be of at least a certain size before it is economically feasible to provide them with a sufficient number of desirable facilities and services. Among these are specialized physical facilities and such personnel as full-time principals, supervisors, nurses, secretaries, and guidance workers. The physical-education program in a four-room neighborhood school will inevitably be different from, and almost certainly inferior to, the program in a larger school equipped with gymnasium, apparatus, and supplies, and the daily services of a physical-education instructor. A twenty-teacher high school cannot possibly offer as much instruction in science, foreign languages, vocational subjects, and the arts as can a high school with sixty or eighty teachers.

Second, the larger the school becomes, the greater becomes the need to provide some sort of mechanism for creating family-size subunits within the total building. In the "house plan" in secondary schools, for example, several hundred pupils are housed together in the same wing of a large building or in a separate building in a campus-type school. A housemaster and a nucleus faculty group experience with the pupils some degree of autonomy and privacy. Similarly, some of the team-teaching projects, both in elementary schools and secondary schools, have had the effect of creating a "school-within-a-school" in which a smaller and more intimate group of fellow-students can enjoy opportunities and satisfactions that might not be available in a larger, more impersonal setting. Thus, while extremely large schools built in the interest of economy or efficiency may suffer serious drawbacks, imaginative internal organization may make it possible to preserve at least some of the privileges and advantages associated with smaller schools.

Clearly, "optimum" school size is difficult to define. When planners discuss the size of any existing school or any future school, they must inevitably consider such matters as pupil travel and safety, the financial capacity of the community, the availability of land, and local demographic trends. Large, congested cities, for example, may have no real alternative to building very large schools on small sites. Conversely, sparsely populated rural areas cannot possibly operate large schools, because pupils would have to travel too great a distance to reach them. Sometimes, too, the layouts of highways or industrial developments force a community to plan schools in certain neighborhoods regardless of the size of its potential pupil population.

Wherever a real choice is possible, elementary schools should be large enough so that all the necessary services and facilities (especially the services of a full-time principal) can be provided, and either small enough or well enough endowed with specialized spaces (such as a library or a playroom) so that each class or team can have regular access to them. (The same problem of access to facilities may exist in high schools, where often there is only one small library and such limited gymnasium space that only the varsity athletes have what amounts to enough exercise.) Moreover, the larger the school, the greater should be the effort to ensure that each subgroup of pupils has both the privacy and the attention it needs. As one enlightened superintendent said in support of his high-school "house plan," each pupil in the school should be in a position to know and be known by at least a significant portion of the faculty, including an administrative officer who has the power to make decisions that affect that pupil and who knows the pupil personally.

HORIZONTAL AND VERTICAL ORGANIZATION

Each school district must decide what school units the child will pass through from the time he first enrolls as a five-year-old until he finally leaves, some twelve or thirteen years later. The district is responsible for regulating the upward (i.e., vertical) progress of the youngster through the school program, and it is also responsible for arranging for the child's current (i.e., horizontal) classification and status at each stage along the way.

The term *vertical organization* is used to describe the policies and procedures by which a school system indicates the child's progress and status during each successive year of schooling. The nearly universal pattern of vertical organization for the past hundred years has been that of the *graded* school: a twelve-year package of subject matter, divided into twelve separate segments stacked on top of each other vertically—that is, from the beginning (at the bottom) to the end (at the top). Each year's (or grade's) work is seen as an entity, and the program follows the calendar of the academic year in evenly proportioned segments. Although at its best the program is responsive to the varying needs and interests of the pupils, there are definite grade-level expectancy standards; any deviation from those standards, either downward or upward, is disapproved. The child whose achievement is below standard is required to spend another year in the same grade; the child who proves capable of advancing at a faster rate is permitted to "skip a grade." All other children are expected to conform to the grade timetable and adhere to the specified curriculum sequence. Report cards, or equivalent devices to indicate the quantity and quality of each child's school performance, are usually geared in some direct way to grade-level-expectancy standards, as are the standardized tests upon which evaluative judgments are made.

Alternatives to the strictly graded classroom have been under consideration for at least seventy-five years. Over the past sixty years, projects in school reorganization (such as the Winnetka Plan, the Dalton Plan, and others described in chapter five) have had as their goal the modification or the elimination of the graded structure. In chapter four, where we discuss the so-called nongraded school, we shall describe such attempted modifications in detail. For the moment, we may list the following alternatives to the strictly graded classroom.

1. The preservation of the graded-school labels and machinery for administrative convenience, but with an effort to provide for each child a greater degree of program flexibility in the grade to which he is assigned.

2. The more-or-less automatic "promotion" of each class of pupils to each successive grade, with the understanding that in some cases the actual achievement of the pupil is not up to the standard theoretically required in that grade.

3. The assignment of pupils to a class that embraces two or more grades—the so-called multigrade classroom—in which it is therefore somewhat easier for each child to work at his appropriate "grade level" in each of the various content areas.

4. The official abandonment of the whole graded structure along with its vocabulary and its machinery in favor of the so-called nongraded arrangements.

Notice that patterns 1 and 2 are similar; the second is merely a more direct admission that graded structure is not a realistic arrangement for all children. In pattern 3, the multigraded classroom, the teacher is confronted with a complicated teaching situation in which each class is composed of youngsters of two or more age levels and an even greater range of achievement levels. And yet this very range creates more opportunities for the teacher to fit above-average and below-average children into appropriate subgroups.

Multigraded class groupings, then, tend to produce a more individualized instructional program than do patterns 1 and 2, in which the pupils are consistently reminded of their grade status. Certain aspects of patterns 1 and 2 can of course be combined with the multigrade idea. In the next chapter, we shall review the arguments favoring the nongraded pattern over these alternatives. We might further observe here, in passing, that *rigid* graded structure seems almost to have vanished from the American educational scene, with alternatives 1 (which we might term "evolutionary subversion of gradedness") and 2 (which is sometimes labeled "social promotion" or "continuous progress") predominating at the present time. The very existence and prevalence of these several alternatives are in themselves convincing testimony that rigid graded structure no longer enjoys the confidence of American teachers.

Horizontal organization—that is, the manner in which a school distributes the children within the school building at any given moment in time—is only indirectly related to the school's choice of graded, multigraded, modified-graded, or nongraded organization. These vertical patterns may be found in combination with any one of the horizontal arrangements in common use today: self-contained classrooms, departmentalized classrooms, cooperative teaching plans, and variants of these three.

Until fairly recently, the self-contained classroom was the most popular form of horizontal organization in the elementary schools. One teacher, a generalist by training and desire, accepted responsibility for all curriculum areas and devoted her full time and attention to a single class of pupils in a room assigned exclusively to them. Each child had a constant association with that one teacher and with a limited number of fellow students. Until the mid-1950's most of the literature on elementary education emphasized the benefits that would accrue to children in such classrooms, and until the early 1960's virtually all college and university programs for training elementary-school teachers required that teachers be familiar with the content and methods in all subject areas.

By contrast, secondary schools have traditionally been organized into departments, with each teacher responsible for only one subject. In smaller schools, of course, teachers have often been asked to teach two or more subjects; but state laws and employers' preferences have required that in such cases the teacher should have had at least an academic minor or its equivalent in the subjects taught.

At various times over the past half-century, the departmentalized arrangement has been used in elementary schools as well as in secondary schools. Many private elementary schools have long been organized into departments, especially in grades 4 and above, and experimentation with such variations as "semidepartmentalization" has kept the idea active. On the whole, however, departmentalization has been unpopular among elementary-school educators.

Coincident with the emergence of team teaching in the 1950's, and probably drawing its energy from the same motivating forces and conditions, was a strong trend toward some form of academic specialization and training-in-depth for elementary teachers. As knowledge increases and methodologies become more complex, even the teacher of very young children finds it difficult to pose as a "master of all contents." Research carried on in team-organized and departmentalized elementary schools has revealed that pupils in such schools are at least as well adjusted as pupils in self-contained classrooms. Moreover, the American public has grown more and more insistent that teacher-training institutions become more rigorous in their academic requirements. Thus, pressure has come from many sides to abandon the self-contained classroom at the elementary level.

Actually, changes in the personnel structure of the elementary school have made the term *self-contained-classroom teacher* somewhat less accurate than it once was. There has been a growing tendency to add trained librarians and other materials specialists to the school staff. And, depending in part on the wealth of the school district, there may also be a number of other full-time or part-time specialists: teachers of music, both vocal and instrumental; teachers of arts and crafts; physical-education instructors; teachers of special education; specialists in remedial services of various types; guidance and testing personnel; and others. The child therefore deals with a number of teachers in addition to his "regular" teacher, who is obliged to coordinate all the experiences he has in school. As a result, some have suggested that the term *coordinating teacher* replace *self-contained-classroom teacher* in elementary-school parlance.

Conventional departmentalization is itself a form of self-contained organization, at least with respect to the teacher's role. Teachers in departmentalized schools have been almost literally autonomous—that is, self-contained—and each of their various assignments has been as independent of the others as are those of self-contained-classroom teachers. The chief difference between the two conventional patterns lies less in the distinction between self-contained and departmentalized than in the distinction between the generalist and the specialist. Most authorities would probably concede that the departmentalized school gives more competent instruction *area by area*. Until recently, however, it was generally believed that the advantages of expert instruction were offset by the uncoordinated and fragmentary experiences the child receives at the hands of independent teachers each unaware of his colleagues' work and each seeing only a limited aspect of the child's growth and performance.

The emergence of cooperative teaching, in which there is presumably greater coordination and communication among several cooperating colleagues, has given a fresh impetus to the idea of specialized teaching. In this third type of horizontal organization we find some of the advantages associated with both self-containment and departmentalization. An arrangement that allows each teacher to work in the area for which he is specially trained and that at the same time obliges him to take into account the contributions and experiences of his fellow teachers enables the school to "have its cake and eat it too!"

So far in our discussion of horizontal organization we have focused on the role of the teacher under one plan or another. Now we shall turn to the various ways of organizing the curriculum and of grouping pupils.

For several decades secondary schools have shown interest in the "core curriculum" (other phrases are also used to describe it), in which two or more subjects are combined and taught in a "core." Often two teachers, one an English specialist and one a social-studies specialist, work together with a group of students within a two-period time block. The students may be grouped heterogeneously. Or they may be grouped homogeneously, on the basis of some such criterion as academic ability, academic achievement, age, interest and motivation, or presumed "teachability." The teachers may elect to work in tandem, or to pursue their respective fields separately for the most part, or to carry on both joint activities and separate ones.

Sometimes the secondary school will organize part of its curriculum around some broad problem or topic that embraces a number of content areas. Again, the staff must decide how the pupils are to be grouped and how the teachers are to integrate their efforts.

Sometimes the secondary school will organize part of its curriculum around some broad problem or topic that embraces a number of content areas. Again, the staff must decide how the pupils are to be grouped and how the teachers are to integrate their efforts.

Usually, however, the secondary school organizes its curriculum by subject matter, with one or more teachers in charge of each of the subject areas or departments. Each subject is broken down into successive levels of difficulty, with each level ordinarily associated with a grade level (or its equivalent). The pupils who advance to each level are then subdivided into class groups (or teams) on the basis of either homogeneity or heterogeneity.

In both the elementary and the secondary school, the problem of horizontal classification, placement, and grouping of pupils is one of the most difficult with which the staff is confronted.

PUPIL GROUPING: A POINT OF VIEW

Several times in the last few pages we referred to homogeneous and heterogeneous groupings. In education these terms are used rather loosely. Human beings are so diverse and complicated that exact sameness is almost nonexistent even between identical twins. However, educators find the word *homogeneous* useful in discussions of pupil grouping to indicate a presumed similarity between two or more children that may justify dealing with them in essentially the same way. Conversely, they use the term *heterogeneous* as a label for groups that contain persons who are dissimilar in some important respect.

Discussions of homogeneous versus heterogeneous grouping have usually been in terms of (1) how best to establish permanent class groups or teams and (2) how best to organize *subgroups* of learners *within* the class or team. In the latter case, the subgroups are often regarded as temporary and specific to a given task or topic; here it may not be very serious if the teacher makes an error assigning a pupil to the group. Much of the time, however, subgroups within a class (for example, the all-important "reading group" to which an elementary-school child is assigned) are relatively permanent; here an error in the teacher's judgment could be disastrous. The same is true of the class or the team to which the pupil is permanently assigned.

Many schools deliberately assign pupils at random to the various classes at each grade level or within each subject. Sometimes they follow this policy in order to protect themselves against the charge that they have exercised some sort of discrimination or prejudice against the child. If there are three fifth-grade classes in a school, and if the "top" students are placed in one class, the "average" in another, and the poorer students in another, the parents of the pupils in the last two classes are likely to share with their children a sense of frustration, disappointment, or worse. The fear of stigmatizing poor students and the hesitancy to set up an "elite" class have inhibited school officials from trying to establish homogeneous class groups. Somewhat the same situation prevails in junior and senior high schools, though in the senior high schools the very nature of the curriculum and of course selections tends to create relatively homogeneous class groups.

Another deterrent to the effort to establish homogeneous class groups has been that homogeneity is at best a single-criterion proposition. In the elementary school, the "high" class groups usually comprise the most efficient or successful *readers,* with the least efficient in the "low" groups. Often, the groups are far less homogeneous in terms of arithmetic, or science, or any other subject. Ironically, however, teachers sometimes deal with the children as if they were indeed all high, average, or low in every respect. This is yet another reason for the resentment some parents show to homogeneous class groups. It would probably be better for educators to stop referring to groups as simply "homogeneous" and always use a modifier ("homogeneous in reading ability," "homogeneous in mental age," "homogeneous in spelling aptitude") whenever they refer to a class or group in which similarity exists.

What instructional advantages or disadvantages accompany various patterns of class grouping? At the risk of oversimplification, we might approach this question by asking another: What does the pupil need in order to profit from his associations with his fellow pupils? Although learning is ultimately a personal matter, there are several ways in which being a member of a group contributes to learning. One is reinforcement. A pupil who is striving to solve a problem or to understand an idea may receive both direct and indirect assistance from the pupils who are working alongside him. If they are equally interested in completing the task, if they are equally able (within broad limits, of course) to comprehend or deal with its elements, and if they bring similar histories and backgrounds to it, then when one pupil suddenly discovers a clue or expresses a vaguely conceived idea in a clarifying way, the others easily share in his discovery. In short, the fact that all the pupils are similar in certain pertinent respects makes it possible for them to learn together. It is not so much that they have learned *from* one another, but rather that they have been able to behave almost as if they were one person. This is the "homogeneous group" at its best.

Sometimes, however, association with other pupils may bestow on the learner an advantage of quite a different kind. Many of the things a child needs to know, to feel, and to do demand that he realign and modify the ideas, convictions, and perspectives he has built up over time. These may include attitudes toward persons of greater or lesser talent, of broader or narrower background, of more or less maturity, and so on. Some feelings and ideas we can learn only from people who are unlike ourselves. Two children who have lived under the same roof with the same parents have less to teach each other about family life, parental behavior, and the home as a physical or social environment than do two children from different families. A child who has visited France probably has more to learn from a child who has lived in Brazil than from one who has also visited France. A child who has never known hunger will learn more about life through conversation with a classmate from a poverty-stricken home than from other children at the country club.

In short, the heterogeneity that is so abundantly present in every class or group of pupils is one of the great assets that the group possesses. By assembling pupils of varied talents and backgrounds and encouraging interactions that enable them to contribute ideas, feelings, perceptions, and experiences to one another, we can add a great deal to the lives and the development of them all. Not only that, but we probably contribute to the strength and the morale of the community by creating bonds of friendship and understanding between children who may as adults follow many different paths.

In general, American teachers have had more confidence and experience in working with approximately homogeneous classes and groups then they have had with deliberately heterogeneous groups. Curricula in which there is provision for common experiences shared by children of varying ages and capacities are still relatively rare. Therefore, as it becomes more evident that such experiences are an important component of intellectual and personal growth, it is to be hoped that teachers will throw their energies into this challenging new curriculum frontier.

CLASS AND GROUP SIZE

As we have said, the problem of grouping has to do with both the larger group to which the pupil belongs throughout the year and the various subgroups to which he belongs through the day. Before cooperative teaching emerged as an alternative to self-contained or departmentalized classes, discussions of fixed-class membership were usually linked to the question of optimum class size.

Most authorities agreed that the optimum number of children with whom each pupil lived in the classroom throughout the year should be twenty, twenty-five, or thirty. But debate on this matter was as heated as debate on the question of the optimum type of class—that is, heterogeneous or homogeneous. Research into the question of optimal class size never produced any significant findings.

The basic, relatively stable group of peers to which the pupil belongs throughout the year may be described as his "school family." In the elementary school there is usually only one such family for each child. In a departmentalized secondary school the pupil may belong to more than one family: one for mathematics, one for English, and so on. In the past, each family had just one adult head (the teacher, acting in an independent parental role). Therefore the optimum family size coincided with the number of pupils over whom one teacher could reasonably exercise control and influence in a personal way.

Over the years, educators came to regard as desirable a ratio of one teacher to every twenty or thirty children. And somewhere along the way a mystique began to develop around those numbers, not only in relationship to the teacher's capacity but also in relationship to the morale and health of the pupil group itself. Soon educators began to impute all sorts of interpersonal and social advantages to the class size that had proved (for altogether different reasons) to be practical, and the class of twenty-five became accepted as ideal.

For these and related reasons, team teaching and other arrangements calling for larger instructional groups met with a hostile reception in their early years. By the mid-1960's, however, educators had become more willing to examine the question of class size, along with the question of grouping, in a more objective manner.

It will be many years before firm answers to some of these questions emerge. Available data suggest, however, that class groups of twenty to thirty may in fact be among the least desirable and the least efficient of all possible sizes!

To justify this conclusion, let us consider the types of activity in which pupils are likely to engage in a modern school program.

Independent Study.   The educational reform movement rides on the concept of "individualized instruction." All the major curriculum projects assume and provide for a large amount of independent and self-directed study. Teaching machines, tape recorders, and other technological innovations offer the child a highly individualized sequence of lessons at which he works privately on his own time schedule. Libraries and study centers are becoming ever more prominent in school building and program planning. Language laboratories and special project areas are enabling pupils to work apart from other children (psychologically, if not physically). Some schools are even providing private study space for their pupils, equivalent in a sense to the private office of the adult world. In the school of the future, much of the program will be geared to the self-directing, self-supervising, independent learner—a group of one!

Closely related to independent study is tutorial instruction. Teachers have always found it desirable to set aside a certain amount of time for a face-to-face, one-to-one relationship with the child. One reason for the persistent loyalty to low teacher-pupil ratios has been the recognized need for paying individual attention to each child. Whether for routine functions or for highly charged encounters as in counseling, these one-to-one meetings of the child and the teacher have happened all too infrequently. In the school of the future, especially as independent study becomes more extensive, it will be all the more necessary to provide time for them.

Working and Interacting. Available evidence on the optimum size of a working group suggests that the group must be small, certainly much smaller than the class of twenty to twenty-five. Working and interacting groups seem to work best when they are limited to about six members (but they can be effective with as few as five and as many as eight members). Good cooperative work, one prominent psychologist has asserted, is simply impossible when there are more than eight pupils in the group.

This might seem like a difficult number to arrange in the typical school. But we must remember that working groups do not usually require the constant supervision of the teacher; if suitable space is provided, four or more groups can operate simultaneously under the supervision of one teacher. The trend toward individualized instruction will probably require an ever-increasing use of these small, working, interacting subgroups of the class in the schools of the future.

Discussing and Decision-making. When people of any age—children or adults—come together to discuss some intellectual problem and to arrive at a decision, the available evidence suggests that their efficiency will decline sharply if more than twelve persons are involved. Twelve—the size of a jury—seems to be the "right" size for a discussion group. Under some circumstances the number might be stretched to fifteen. But to resort to the far more typical numbers of twenty, twenty-five, thirty, or more means, if we have read the evidence correctly, sacrificing a great deal of the potential value of the experience.

Here we encounter the first real irony in our data. For years on end, teachers have been conducting discussions with classes of twenty to thirty, and they have become more or less accustomed— we might even say resigned—to the level of success that is possible with groups of that size. In retrospect, it would seem that the discussions usually involved only about twelve of the pupils, while the rest sat by as spectators! It is hoped that the future will see a change in practice, with discussion groups rarely exceeding twelve to fifteen.

Attending, Viewing, Listening, and Receiving. At one time, pupils spent a great amount of time as a total class, paying attention to what was being presented by the teacher, by a fellow student, by a radio or phonograph, or by some other source of information.

In such instances, the pupil's main responsibility was to absorb and remember the ideas and events being presented. This approach to teaching still predominates in many college classes, and although it can be overused with public-school children, there are times when it is altogether appropriate for the teacher or some other person to tell, show, or demonstrate something to the class. In other words, lectures and demonstrations do have a proper place in the scheme of things, and pupils can profit from situations in which their participation is limited to "their eyes and their ears." Educational television is among the forms such instruction may take, as are the various arrangements referred to as "large-group instruction."

How large the group should be depends on (1) the nature of the lesson and the conditions under which it can be presented and (2) the number of children within the potential total audience for whom the lesson in question is assuredly relevant. Large-group lessons depend on the instructional space and equipment available and also on the ease and comfort with which the potential audience is able to see and hear what is happening. The size of any given audience will depend in part on the size of the school population, a small school obviously having fewer children from whom each potential audience can be selected.

Large-group instruction could be directed to almost any number of pupils. If we agree that fifteen is the maximum for discussion groups, then we could reasonably argue that sixteen and beyond is a large group. In most schools, the number actually assembled for such instruction is more likely to be forty to two hundred.

In summary, we have identified four major types of activities in which pupils of the elementary or secondary school are likely to engage. Two of them might for convenience be labeled as *small-group instruction,* and we have prescribed definite limitations on the number involved in accordance with the function of the group. One, labeled *large-group instruction,* operates only under such limitations as practicability and relevance may require: if only twenty-nine children in the school are ready at this moment for the lesson in question, then the large group is twenty-nine; if a million or more children are ready, as might be the case for educational television in a metropolitan area, then the large group is one million.

Some educators have wondered what fraction of the child's school

life ought to be spent in each of the aforementioned activities.
J. Lloyd Trump, a pioneer in educational reform and Director
of the Commission on the Experimental Study of the Utilization
of the Staff in the Secondary School,[2] has recommended that about
40 percent of the student's time be spent in large classes, another
40 percent in individual study, and 20 percent in small-group discussion. He recommends further that more flexible schedules, more
appropriate physical spaces, more appropriate curriculum planning and coordination, and more effective use of teacher talents
should accompany the recommended grouping arrangements.

These suggestions are consistent with those made by a group of
educators who helped plan a new "middle school" to accommodate
pupils from eleven to fourteen years of age (in old-fashioned terminology, pupils of grades 6, 7, and 8). This group recommended
the following allotments:

1. Independent pupil activities   20–25%
2. Teacher and pupil in a tutorial relationship   5%
3. Working, interacting groups (five to eight pupils)   25%
4. Discussion, decision-making groups (nine to fifteen pupils)   30%
5. Large-group lessons   15–20%

The group further recommended that, after a decade or so of experience with the new pattern of grouping, there might be a slight
reduction in the time allocated to the nine- to fifteen-pupil discussion groups with a proportionate increase in time for five- to
eight-pupil working groups, the large-group lessons, and the independent activities.

Arranging the child's school life along these lines should provide a good balance among activities in which he is largely a viewer
or listener, activities in which he enjoys the give-and-take of
group life, and activities that permit him and his teacher to deepen
their understanding of each other.

SCHOOL AND CLASS ORGANIZATION: A SUMMARY

In this chapter we have tried to bring together a variety of ideas
that bear upon the important topic of school and class organization. We have drawn certain conclusions, from research and educational history, to the effect that the conventional ways of organ-

2. Sponsored by The National Association of Secondary School Principals of the
   NEA and supported by the Ford Foundation and the Fund for the Advancement of Education.

izing schools and classes are by no means sacred, that they are, in fact, in some ways undesirable. We have suggested that every community should feel free to experiment with alternative patterns. The educational reform movement has revealed many new and unfamiliar ways of defining the size and structure of school units, and what seem to be better ways of organizing the school both vertically and horizontally are now gaining acceptance. The need for each child to have continuous contact with other children, both similar and dissimilar to him, has become more clear. We have argued that the child needs various types of relationships with other pupils, with materials of instruction, and with teachers. The necessity for reexamining conventional beliefs about class size and pupil grouping has been brought into focus. In these and related matters, we have shown that variety and flexibility are absolutely necessary.

It is impossible to predict whether the school of the future will settle on a particular combination of vertical and horizontal organizational arrangements or whether many different combinations will coexist. The succeeding chapters will describe two patterns that seem especially deserving of adoption: formally structured, hierarchically organized team teaching and the full-fledged, nongraded school. Even if these ideas are universally adopted, however, school staffs will probably employ several different ways of implementing them.

The figure suggests the great variety of school and class organization patterns already in use in the United States. It is of necessity incomplete (for example, it ignores the possibilities of homogeneous and heterogeneous grouping), but it shows various combinations of the possible patterns. Boxes 1 through 8 have as a constant element the self-contained classroom; in boxes 9 through 16, the constant element is informal cooperative organization; in boxes 17 through 24, team teaching is the constant element. All the boxes in the top half of the figure represent some form of nongradedness; all the boxes in the bottom half are graded. Each horizontal pair of boxes shows two alternatives in age grouping: the lefthand box in each case refers to children of the same age, and the righthand box refers to interage groups.

Box 18 (nongrading combined with team teaching and multiage grouping) represents the theoretical ideal. By implication, box 7 represents the theoretically least desirable combination. The reader might test his own beliefs by trying to determine which combinations of horizontal and vertical organization seem to him the *next best* and the *next worst* arrangements, assuming for the moment that he, too, sees boxes 18 and 7 as the two extremes. He might also try to answer a strategic question. Assume that a school is presently organized along the lines suggested by box 7. Assume, further, that the staff of the school decides that box 18 is the ideal toward which it would like to move, but that it wants

FNG ① UAG SCO	FNG ② MAG SCO	FNG ⑨ UAG ICO	FNG ⑩ MAG ICO	FNG ⑰ UAG TT	FNG ⑱ MAG TT
NNG ③ UAG SCO	NNG ④ MAG SCO	NNG ⑪ UAG ICO	NNG ⑫ MAG ICO	NNG ⑲ UAG TT	NNG ⑳ MAG TT
MG ⑤ UAG SCO	MG ⑥ MAG SCO	MG ⑬ UAG ICO	MG ⑭ MAG ICO	MG ㉑ UAG TT	MG ㉒ MAG TT
FG ⑦ UAG SCO	FG ⑧ MAG SCO	FG ⑮ UAG ICO	FG ⑯ MAG ICO	FG ㉓ UAG TT	FG ㉔ MAG TT

(vertical axis label: Toward the Ideal)

⟶ Toward the Ideal ⟶

FG Formally graded. Relatively rigid adherence to grade-level-expectancy standards. "Promotion" and "failure" are used, along with A–B–C–D–E–F report cards.

MG Modified graded. The vocabulary of the graded school is still in use, but teachers are attempting to provide for individual differences.

NNG Nominal nongradedness. The vocabulary of the graded school has been rejected, but vestiges of graded structure are still in evidence.

FNG Full-fledged nongradedness. Teachers have succeeded in stamping out the undesirable features of the graded school.

UAG Unit-age grouping. Children in the class or team are all of approximately the same age (e.g., all seven-year-olds).

MAG Multiage or interage grouping. Children in the class or team are of two or more ages (e.g., nine- and ten-year-olds).

SCO Self-contained classroom organization (one autonomous teacher).

ICO Informal cooperative organization. Several autonomous teachers working informally together (e.g., cooperative departmentalization, semidepartmentalization, shared responsibilities, pupil interchange, combining of classes).

TT Team teaching, formally organized.

to make that move in a series of steps over perhaps four or five years. To which box ought the staff make its first move? Which box after that?

Perhaps the best way to approach this strategic question is to consider the various characteristics of the two major ideas, team teaching and nongrading, which are likely to influence such a decision.

*Suggestions for Class Discussion
and Further Investigation*

1. A new community is being planned in a rural area lying between two major cities. The state and local school officials have said that they want to create a "model school" program in this new community, based on the best knowledge and skill available. If you were an educational consultant, what would be your recommendations on school unit organization, school size, and related general policies? What policies would you recommend to ensure that first-rate teachers would apply for positions in the new schools? (See chapters one and two.)

2. This chapter has discussed both homogeneous and heterogeneous groupings. What are some specific lessons or experiences that seem appropriate within each of these two contexts?

3. At one point in the chapter it was suggested that groups of twenty to thirty pupils may be the least efficient and least desirable of all possible group sizes. Accept this premise for the purpose of discussion, and ask yourself how school buildings ought to be designed in view of that premise.

4. The percentages indicated on page 40 are not appropriate for all kinds of lessons or content areas, but they represent an overall average. Several educators have argued that certain content areas—for example, science at the 4–5–6 grade level—can be taught chiefly through large-group lessons. Others feel that certain subjects or topics should never be taught in large groups. What is your opinion?

Suggestions for Further Reading

In John I. Goodlad's *Planning and Organizing for Teaching*, Washington, D.C.: NEA, 1963, there is an excellent discussion of horizontal and vertical organization. Also helpful are two chapters contributed by John Goodlad and Robert Anderson to The Sixty-first Yearbook of the National Society for the Study of Education, Part I: *Individualizing Instruction,* Chicago: Univ. of Chicago Press, 1962. Also in the Yearbook, Part II: *The Changing American School,* Chicago: Univ. of Chicago Press, 1966, there is an article by Glen Heathers, "School Organization: Nongrading, Dual Progress, and Team Teaching," which is worth reading as well. Also of interest is the article "Unscrambling the Vocabulary of School Organization," by John Goodlad and Kenneth Rehage, in *NEA Journal,* 51 (November 1962), pp. 34–36.

Though published in 1957, Alexander J. Stoddard's *Schools for Tomorrow: An Educator's Blueprint,* New York: Fund for the Advancement of Education, remains a timely statement about class size and school organization. The writings of J. Lloyd Trump, *Focus on Change: Guide to Better Schools,* with Dorsey Baynham, Chicago: Rand McNally, 1961, and *Images of the Future,* Washington, D.C.: National Association of Secondary-School Principals of the NEA, 1959, also remain pertinent.

Chapter Four

Innovations in Organization:
Theory and Practice
in the Nongraded School

Our essential arguments to this point have been, in brief, that:
(1) the very essence of the American Dream is that each individual is enabled to reach the peak of his inborn potential in all
dimensions of life, including the intellectual; (2) there is such
great diversity within and between individuals that (among other
implications) the inborn potential power of each individual is
notably different from that of all others; (3) for a variety of reasons,
including the rigidity and inflexibility of schools as they have been
organized, the dream of fulfilling each person's potential has been
far from realized; (4) there is good reason to believe that a more
flexible school arrangement, operating more efficiently and reasonably, could help to close the gap between aspiration and actuality;
and (5) various organizational changes with greater built-in flexibility are therefore a necessary aspect of the educational reform
movement.

We have seen that the vertical organization of a school may be
based on the conventional graded structure or on the so-called
nongraded structure, or on some modification of either or both.
Periodically, the school must make some kind of official reference
to the current status of the pupil within the total school program,
which usually lasts for twelve or thirteen years. For the past hundred years, schools have commonly done so by means of the terminology and administrative machinery associated with the graded
structure. Moreover, they have used this structure in setting up the
course of study, with each grade directly related to a specific body
of subject matter. The sequential order was presumed to represent the average levels of potential achievement for each successive
age group.

The graded school was developed during a century when teachers were poorly educated and poorly trained and when the cur-

45

riculum itself was poorly organized and unstructured. There was a real need for packaging the school program into explicit and sequential portions over each of which a teacher could achieve mastery. Consequently, gradedness served a highly useful purpose and made a great contribution to educational development. In fact, it may be no exaggeration to say that the graded school of the nineteenth century was in large measure responsible for America's emergence as a major world power in the twentieth century.

Over the years, however, it has become apparent that the graded school was based on false and even dangerous assumptions about the structure of knowledge and about human learning. The insights presently available to American teachers render obsolete and invalid the whole concept of expecting each child of a given age to conform to arbitrarily defined grade-level expectancies.

In the graded school of old, teachers tended to believe that all children of a given age were capable of mastering the prescribed work of the grade to which they were assigned, subject only to their willingness to accept responsibility for mastering it. Influenced by theological interpretations of will and morality, many teachers sincerely believed that a child's failure to attain the grade-level standard was somehow immoral. So it seemed quite fitting that he should suffer punishment in the form of a low mark and eventually a nonpromotion or, in the literal vocabulary of gradedness, a failure.

Similarly, precociousness in children was something to be feared, because it frustrated the teacher's desire to keep her pupils working at a uniform pace. Books on education written during the mid-nineteenth century even went so far as to suggest that precocious pupils were potentially mischievous and therefore to be "kept in their proper place" at all costs.

This argument seems to have survived into the twentieth century, since in literally graded schools some teachers are still loath to allow their brighter students to move along to textbooks of a higher grade. They prefer, instead, to keep such children busy with additional, often unnecessary, work at their current grade. Sometimes, ironically, this is done under the reassuring name of "enrichment," which to the bright child is often nothing more than repetition and practice in skills that he has already mastered. Teachers who behave in this manner do, perhaps, avoid the embarrassment of having the teacher of the next grade level complain that the children have already read or done what she planned for them. And they manage to avoid the complicated planning problems that arise when the members of a class become widely separated in achievement.

This is not to indict such teachers or even to imply that all graded teachers in the last century followed this practice. But it does seem that the pedagogical viewpoint based on the relatively primitive knowledge about human learning and motivation available before 1900 often resulted in what we would now regard as cruel and crude treatment of the child.

Even before the turn of the century, the rigidity and the illogic of the lock-step graded school were attacked by educators who argued for greater flexibility and more enlightened pedagogical principles. Among the results of their efforts were the St. Louis and Pueblo plans of the late nineteenth century and the Batavia Plan, the Winnetka Plan, the Dalton Plan, John Dewey's Laboratory School, the Eight Year Study, and such related phenomena as the Montessori schools and the more recent surge of special programs for gifted children. Many other efforts of this sort left no trace at all.

Over the past half-century there has been a distressingly slow but steady erosion of the literally graded school. This erosion has been represented by such practices as "automatic promotion," "social promotion," and other schemes that blunted the worst features of gradedness while preserving some of its outward forms. More recently, particularly since about 1955, the profession has rejected outright even the outward forms of gradedness and has advocated an antigraded philosophy. The somewhat unimaginative word *nongraded,* or its synonym *ungraded,* is heard over and over again in discussions of flexible vertical organization.

Sometimes semantic confusion or disparities in perception make these discussions frustrating and fruitless. Those who favor nongraded schools tend, as does the present author, to use adjectives like "rigid," "lock-step," and "inflexible" when referring to graded schools and, conversely, to reserve for nongradedness all the complimentary phrases. Often this tendency has prompted the angry rejoinder that existing schools are being maligned, that in fact the modern graded school has a great deal more flexibility and is more responsive to children's needs than its critics realize.

This reaction has a certain plausibility. In the climate of the 1960's, it is hard to believe that very many teachers in graded classrooms are adhering rigidly to the grade-level timetable and are brow-beating children who are "behind schedule." However, in America there are still teachers who are so sadistic and ill motivated that they dangle the Damoclean sword of nonpromotion over the heads of their pupils. There are still graded classrooms in which below-average children are not being encouraged to work with the more manageable materials of a lower grade level. Many grade teachers still hesitate to give their brighter pupils at least an occasional opportunity to savor ideas and materials that are usually identified with a higher grade. In short, there are still graded classrooms in which the teacher is literally and rigidly adhering to gradedness.

Clearly gradedness is still a powerful and destructive force in American schools and in the American culture. There persists a nineteenth-century conviction that grade-related reward and punishment are effective stimuli to effort, and the curriculum guidebooks and sequences that have crystallized over many years of graded organization are still distressingly dear to the hearts of many teachers and administrators. Such anachronisms as the A–B–C–D–E–F report still prevail; many textbooks continue to be printed with their grade designations plainly visible on the covers; curriculum writers continue to refer constantly to "first grade" and "fifth grade"; test manufacturers continue to publish all their materials (scoring codes, summary sheets, manuals) in terms of grade-level–expectancy standards; and nearly all the educational reports emanating from local, state, and national agencies continue to remind the public of the graded structure of the schools. Less than one third of the elementary schools in the country and less than 2 percent of the secondary schools have announced their intention to depart in some significant way from this pattern. In short, the educational profession in America seems to be dragging its heels in putting the obsolete, inflexible graded school into the historical museum where it belongs.

WHY SO SLOW?

What are the reasons for this slow progress? One reason is that some teachers and educational leaders are ignorant of available child-development information, technically incompetent, or lacking in professional motivation. A more sympathetic explanation is that any serious effort invoked by a nongraded philosophy to individualize instruction and to achieve the school atmosphere raises huge problems of curriculum revision, technological development, administrative invention, and professional retraining. Finally, the proponents of nongradedness have failed to dramatize the need for major reform and to offer specific guidance to those who are prepared to institute nongraded schools.

Education is a notoriously conservative enterprise, and indeed on many issues it should be. Hesitancy to improve the organization of schools, by contrast with caution about major changes in goals or philosophy, would however seem to be less than defensible in the current context. Any form of organization that prevents us from achieving a philosophic objective such as the realization of each child's innate potential must be modified. No American educator disputes this, nor is any recognized educator currently writing or lecturing *in favor of* the conventional graded school. But American educators have not yet become indignant enough to initiate aggressive and imaginative corrective action.

One reason may be that the present generation of school authorities (the superintendents, principals, supervisors, and curriculum directors), together with the administrators and executives of universities and professional organizations, and the professors who train teachers and administrators, consist of successful alumni of graded schools. Further, since they gained their professional experience in the classroom at a time when the graded structure was still securely established, they are successful practitioners in a conventional context. Their repertoire is a graded repertoire! Understandably, they are either unable or reluctant to espouse the theory and practice of a counterstructure.

Those leaders who have specialized in curriculum development and the preparation of materials in particular have tremendous power either to obstruct change or to facilitate it. Many of them are unfortunately forced by the sheer weight of their workloads to choose between patching up the established program and going full speed ahead into the dangerous waters of total reform. Others whose work is in the field of textbook writing find themselves the psychological prisoners of a well-established and highly competitive textbook industry whose profits are apparently threatened by the trend toward more individualized instruction.

Here, to state a rather blunt truth, is where a great deal of the heel-dragging is going on in education. Already noted is the practice of printing grade labels on the covers or title pages of textbooks. When confronted with the argument that this is a disservice to the nongraded cause, the publisher's usual retort is that teachers and administrators insist on having the grade designation immediately visible. This may be true in some instances, of course, and as such it is a rather devastating comment on the intelligence and the sophistication of such teachers. If a teacher's choice of a book depends on knowing it is a 3^2 reader, rather than on specific familiarity with the book's contents as they relate to his pupils' needs, those pupils are not being well served.

However, the publishers themselves seem eager to maintain visible grade designations. Perhaps they suspect that as nongraded schools become more prevalent the sales of standard textbooks will decline. In community after community, the adoption of more flexible vertical organization has enabled the schools to get along with fewer copies of the standard textbooks, since pupils arrive at each successive academic level on a staggered schedule. Also, the abandonment of the graded structure almost invariably reduces the teacher's dependence on graded textbooks and increases his tendency to use other kinds of books and materials. Although the school may actually be spending more money than before on books, the publishers tend to lose sales in the lucrative field of graded textbooks and are forced into the production of less profitable nonstandardized materials. Small wonder, then, that some of the nationally famous authors who work for the publishers in the textbook field are so often silent when the topic of nongradedness is under discussion.

The success of the nongraded arrangement depends ultimately on the improvement of curriculum. What is especially difficult about running a nongraded school or a nongraded classroom is *not* how to organize the program, or how to group the pupils, or how to report pupil progress to parents, or how to set up recordkeeping systems, or how to help teachers solve the numerous other administrative problems that arise. What *is* difficult is how to solve the *curriculum* problems that the organizational scheme raises.

For example, which skill experiences are best arranged through individualized programs in which pupils can proceed at their own rate of speed, and which experiences are best reserved for groups? What topics, presented under what conditions, are appropriate for classes composed of youngsters whose academic potential and achievements range over a wide spectrum? What kinds of experiences can be shared by youngsters in multiage classes in which a great range of responses and contributions is possible? Just how does a spiral curriculum work? How can we better teach for the process goals? These and other questions bedevil the teachers in nongraded schools. Until our curriculum experts begin to attack these problems and produce specific recommendations that teachers can understand, progress will be at a snail's pace.

Another reason for the slow acceptance of the nongraded concept is that the great majority of pilot programs have been deficient. Most of the efforts at nongrading between 1942 and the mid-1960's can be classified as follows: (1) serious efforts to give the idea full-scale development in a well-conceived form, (2) serious efforts to implement one or more aspects of the nongraded idea in a well-conceived form, (3) modest efforts to achieve nongrading within an inadequate theoretical frame of reference, and (4) fraudulent or naive use of the vocabulary of nongradedness to describe what is in fact a conventional graded program. Fewer than a hundred programs fall into the first category. Among them are the elementary laboratory school under John Goodlad's direction at the University of California in Los Angeles and the Dual Progress Plan developed by George Stoddard of New York University. Not a great many more fall into the second category. The overwhelming majority belong in the third category, and there is an embarrassingly large number in the fourth.

So primitive, in fact, have been the first efforts to develop nongraded schools that Alexander Frazier of Ohio State University complained in 1961 that the nongraded school movement had to be rescued from some of its advocates.

Further confusion results from the fact that whereas gradedness can and does persist in the hearts and actions of teachers even when they are supposedly operating in a nongraded manner, nongradedness as a professional concept can and does operate outside of and in spite of the official organization structure. This raises havoc with research, since often the allegedly nongraded experimental group is in fact just as graded as the control group. If the researchers were to examine the operation and the atmosphere more carefully, they might discover that the nominally graded groups were more faithful to the ideals of nongradedness than the pilot nongraded programs with which they are being compared.

Another problem in field research is that the researchers ask the wrong questions, use the wrong instruments in trying to answer them, and confine themselves to inappropriate models of analysis and presentation. For example, many researchers have used

standardized achievement test scores to judge the effect or merit
of nongradedness. These tests are often irrelevant to the instructional situation and therefore of little value. They usually deal
only with skill development in reading, English language arts, and
arithmetic; and even in literally graded schools, teaching practices
in these subjects are probably somewhat adjusted to the capacities
of pupils. When teachers shift to a nongraded program, the changes
they make in the first few years in the teaching of reading and
arithmetic are likely to be far less dramatic than are measurable
changes that will take place in the psychological atmosphere of the
school.

For example, the first significant effect of a change to nongradedness may well be an improvement in children's feelings about
school, about the teachers' motives and feelings toward them,
about the reasons for pursuing particular activities and the prospects for success in them, and about their own worth as individuals
and as learners. Further, the children may develop a healthier attitude toward other children and a more realistic and desirable competitive relationship with them. The frictions between age groups
that seem to be encouraged by graded organization may diminish
in measurable ways. Finally, the children's chances for success in
certain areas of the curriculum that are less inherently grade-
structured may improve.

Researchers could gather data on the extent to which flexibility
and adaptability have actually been achieved within the curriculum of a nongraded school, and then they could devise means for
measuring the effect on children. They could interview teachers
or examine their work in an effort to discover how well those
teachers have searched out and made conscious use of data concerning individual needs and progress. And, again, they could study
the consequences of decisions based on such information. They
could examine the type of reporting system in use and its apparent impact on pupil morale and productivity. By assembling similar
data in graded classrooms they could make available to the profession some truly useful data. As it stands, most of the "research
evidence" is essentially worthless. Some notable exceptions can be
found in the work of Maurie Hillson and in a major project sponsored by the New York State Education Department.[1]

1. See L. T. DiLorenzo and Ruth Salter, "Co-operative Research on the Nongraded Primary," *Elementary School Journal*, 65 (February 1965), pp. 269–77.

In summary, then, the recent history of the nongraded school in America is marred by various failures on the part of university professors, school practitioners, research workers, and others to fully comprehend the nature of the movement and what must be done in order to make a fair demonstration possible. When we talk or think about nongradedness, we must remember that there are four arrangements coexisting at the present time:

1. Nominally graded schools and classes in which teachers with a nineteenth-century viewpoint are, without qualms of conscience, behaving as their puritanical predecessors behaved. (We might call them the "original sinners." Happily, the number of such teachers still active in the public schools is very small.)

2. Nominally graded schools and classes in which twentieth-century teachers are mindful of the benefits of nongradedness and therefore use many desirable and flexible procedures. (We might call this group the "bootleggers," because they tend to disregard the laws of gradedness and try to "smuggle in" nongraded practices.)

3. Nominally nongraded schools and classes in which the teachers give little evidence that they really understand or believe in the nongraded concept. (The "underground resistance" might be an appropriate name for these teachers. John Goodlad recently commented, "If only the labels are removed, we have the same old school under a new name and a fraud has been perpetrated.")

4. Nominally nongraded schools and classes in which the teachers are earnestly attempting to live up to the exacting requirements embodied in the concept. (Though the success of many of these teachers has been less than spectacular, we are tempted to call these "the real McCoys," or even "the saints," to contrast them with the sinners' group. Here, of course, is where we would like eventually to be able to classify *all* American educators.)

NONGRADEDNESS AND ITS FORMS

Nongradedness embraces a number of concepts. Perhaps for that reason discussions of the idea have been marred by a tendency to talk about "black versus white," "bad guys versus good guys," and "rigidly graded versus flexibly nongraded." There seems to have been some reluctance to examine the underlying issues and questions.

Nongradedness is a rather unfortunate term, since it refers pri-

marily to what is *not,* rather than to what *is.* Those who use the
term are calling attention to the undesirability and the illegitimacy
of the opposite concept, "gradedness"; consequently their purpose
is essentially antiseptic. In short, they see both the vocabulary of
gradedness and the practices associated with graded vertical organization as evils to be deliberately eliminated. Once that has happened, it may no longer be necessary to use the awkward and nega-
tivistic terminology now used to describe the "good" practices.

Nongradedness refers to two dimensions of the school and its
atmosphere: the philosophy (or the value system) that guides
the behavior of the school staff toward the pupils, and the admin-
istrative-organizational machinery and procedures by means of
which the life of the pupils and teachers is regulated. In short,
nongradedness is both a theoretical proposition and an operational
mechanism. Unlike team teaching, it is not a new staffing pattern.
Unlike educational television, it is not a technological innovation.
Consequently, it is not a component of the curriculum reform
movement, though it may very well be the chief inspiration behind
that movement. Rather, it is a concept of the proper way to provide for children's educational needs and a plan for implementing
that concept.

The many definitions that have been offered differ primarily in
the elegance and the comprehensiveness with which they have
been stated rather than in their conceptual meaning. Without exception, they emphasize the need to individualize instruction and
to develop each individual up to his full potential for physical,
social, intellectual, and civic accomplishment. And without exception they emphasize the need to provide both differentiated *rates*
of pupil progress and variations in the *kinds of program* offered.
Many, though not all, of the definitions refer to the need for more
suitable forms of evaluating and reporting pupil progress, and
most refer to various *means* for individualizing instruction, such
as pupil grouping, independent study, and other procedural arrangements. The titles of nongraded programs differ too. Many
use phrases like "continuous progress plan" or "continuous growth
plan," but others simply refer to the name of the school or city
in such phrases as "The Middletown Project."

Most of the literature on nongradedness talks about early elementary education, and an overwhelming number of the pilot programs are at that level. Actually, however, the movement includes
all levels, from nursery school through the university. Most of the

literature appears in the professional magazines, but there are several complete volumes dedicated to the topic. Most current textbooks on the elementary curriculum devote at least a chapter or part of a chapter to a discussion of the nongraded trend.

In the first major treatment of nongradedness at the secondary-school level, B. Frank Brown of the celebrated Melbourne High School in Florida defined a nongraded school as

> . . . a place which makes arrangements for the individual student to pursue any course in which he is interested, and has the ability to achieve, without regard either to grade level or sequence.[2]

Arguing for inventiveness, flexibility, and quality, Brown discusses the scheduling of students "in a mobile program where they can advance at their own rate," variations in program content, independent study (especially for the more talented students), what he calls a "concept-centered curriculum," and appropriate testing, placement, marking, and reporting practices. The effect of the Melbourne example on secondary-school education has been remarkable.

Other leaders in this field include John Goodlad of the University of California at Los Angeles,[3] Maurie Hillson of Rutgers University, Stuart Dean of the U.S. Office of Education, and George D. Stoddard of New York University, who with Glen Heathers developed the so-called Dual Progress Plan, of which nongraded classes are a major component.

Goodlad, in one of the three major volumes [4] produced by the National Education Association's historic Project on Instruction, pointed out that there are at least three different models of school organization to be found in American schools today. One of these, the graded pattern, grows out of an assumption that schools are intended to cover and to inculcate in pupils a specific body of subject matter; this subject matter is carefully laid out in successive grades and closely identified with those grades. In this pattern, the fact that children differ from one another is an explanation for differences in their performance, not a basis for planning the pro-

---

2. *The Nongraded High School*, Englewood Cliffs, N.J.: Prentice-Hall, 1963, p. 43. See also Brown's more recent book, *The Appropriate Placement School: A Sophisticated Nongraded Curriculum*, West Nyack, New York: Parker Publishing Co., 1965.
3. John I. Goodlad and Robert H. Anderson, *The Nongraded Elementary School*, rev. ed., New York: Harcourt, Brace & World, 1963.
4. *Planning and Organizing for Teaching*, Washington, D.C.: NEA, 1963, p. 190.

gram. Pupils who make slow progress are adjusted to the system by means of nonpromotion.

The second model described by Goodlad represents a kind of in-between stage; his third model has the following characteristics:[5]

1. *School function:* Schools are learner-centered. They are designed to develop the learner as an individual and as a member of society.

2. *Means of fulfilling function:* Focus should be on *ways* of knowing and thinking. Emphasis is on the individual.

3. *Organizational structure:* Graded structure is either ignored as meaningless or replaced by a nongraded plan. Grouping patterns are flexible. Individual differences tend to be accounted for through intraclass provisions rather than interclass provisions.

4. *Individual differences:* Differences in many aspects of development are recognized and used in planning highly individualized programs.

5. *Pupil progress:* Provision is made for both differentiated rates of progress and variations in kinds of program, according to individual needs and abilities.

Multiage Grouping Plans. In *multiage* or *interage* grouping, children of two or more adjoining age levels are assigned to the same team or class. Proponents of this plan argue that children profit socially and intellectually from sharing ideas and problems with children who are different from themselves. This concept was summarized in the title of a pioneering article published in 1957: "By Their Differences They Learn." [6] The article reported on an unusual grouping plan that had been developed in Torrance, California, in which primary classes were composed of approximately ten first-graders, ten second-graders, and ten third-graders, all under the direction of one teacher; intermediate classes were composed of about ten fourth-graders, ten fifth-graders, and ten sixth-graders.

This arrangement demanded that the teachers make more complicated preparations, but it also made it easier for them to provide for fast and slow learners by grouping them with older or younger

5. *Ibid.*, pp. 56–57. See also pp. 65–68.
6. Warren W. Hamilton and Walter Rehwoldt, in *The National Elementary Principal*, 37 (December 1957), pp. 27–29.

children without regard to grade designations. Also, the presence of a wide range of abilities within each class literally forced teachers to study each youngster's needs with greater care than is usually exercised by teachers of single-age graded classes.

One of the effects of the Torrance Plan and of subsequent age experiments was to revitalize research on pupil grouping practices and on the nongraded movement itself. Previously, most nongraded plans had been built on the assumption that homogeneous classes were better both for teachers (fewer preparations to make) and for pupils (competition and interaction only with similar class-mates). Once this assumption had been challenged (fortunately, at a time when cooperative teaching plans were beginning to emerge), educational innovators began to experiment more boldly with patterns that allowed for both heterogeneous and homogeneous subgroupings. Even more dramatic proposals (for example, the deliberate subgrouping of six- and seven-year-olds with early adolescents for specific purposes) are now attracting attention.

Meanwhile, multigrade classes are one of the mechanisms available to those who hope to move into full-fledged nongraded programs. The terms "multiage" and "multigrade" differ only in that the latter implies the continued use of grade labels. Teachers who are hesitant to abandon grade labels and the other machinery of gradedness all at once but who still want greater freedom in providing for individual differences may find multigraded classes or teams an excellent transition. As parents, children, and teachers grow accustomed to the idea, they may become ready for the next logical step: the abandonment of grade labels and the acceptance of nongradedness for the whole group.

The Dual Progress Plan. George Stoddard, convinced that the graded system was obsolete, at least in part, and that specialization in teaching must replace the self-contained, general-purpose class-room, designed a semidepartmentalized approach that has been used primarily in grades 4, 5, and 6. It combines a form of non-gradedness with a modified form of gradedness, and it breaks with certain established patterns of curriculum and instruction.

In Stoddard's Dual Progress Plan, the pupils spend about half the school day in one classroom with a "home teacher" who is a specialist in the teaching of reading and social studies and who performs certain counseling and orientation functions. This half of the day also includes physical education, taught by a physical-education specialist. The home teacher has another section of pupils in the other half of the day. Both sections are labeled fourth grade, fifth grade, or sixth grade. Pupils are promoted to the next grade in this reading–social-studies program (which Stoddard defines as offering the "cultural imperatives" of the society) only when they have satisfied the basic requirements of the grade-level curriculum. It is the teacher's responsibility to know his pupils and their families well, and to this end he works closely with other teachers who deal with the pupils.

Stoddard describes as the "cultural electives" those curriculum areas where society tolerates a wide range of accomplishments: mathematics (aside from the essential arithmetic skills), science, art, and music. The other half of each day is devoted to these subjects. The youngsters are assigned to groups on the basis of achievement and ability without regard to grade level, and they move about from mathematics class to science class and so forth.

About a dozen communities have introduced this plan, in most cases in grades 4, 5, and 6, but in a few instances in grades 3, 7, and 8. The school systems of Ossining and Long Beach in New York conducted a five-year cooperative study between 1958 and 1963, and a fairly extensive literature is now available. Stoddard's definitive volume,[7] several articles and chapters by Heathers, and several publications of the Experimental Teaching Center at New York University constitute a valuable collection of writings in educational research and development, not only because of the intrinsic value of this project but because of the unusual care with which it has been documented.

One of the strengths of the Dual Progress Plan is that it provides an opportunity for specialists to work with elementary-school children. It has failed of complete development, as have nongraded plans and team teaching, largely because of the magnitude of the curriculum problems (or opportunities) that it uncovers, because of administrative complexity, and because of the great difficulties involved in recruiting, training, and retraining teachers with the skills such programs require.

Ultimately, such difficulties are likely to confront all programs that attempt nongrading. The shocking discovery of researchers and innovators has been that the school's successes in individualizing

7. *The Dual Progress Plan,* New York: Harper, 1961, p. 225.

instruction are rare and that teachers are generally ill equipped to meet the demands of the nongraded school.

Nongradedness Beyond the Elementary School. The middle schools that serve what were once known as grades 6, 7, and 8 or 5, 6, 7, and 8 are also tending to adopt nongraded practices. In the past decade a number of "junior high schools" have moved in this direction, and even where the grade labels persist in nominal use it is possible to find many ways in which more individually appropriate school experiences and a more psychologically comfortable school environment have been provided for the youngsters. The rate of change promises to accelerate sharply in the decade ahead.

We have already mentioned Melbourne High School, a striking example of nongradedness at the senior-high level. A major strength of this program is its independent study program. Other excellent examples of programs that feature individualized instruction are Evanston Township High School in Illinois, the two high schools in Newton, Massachusetts, and Theodore High School in Theodore, Alabama (part of the Mobile Public School System).

Although an energetic commitment to full-fledged nongradedness can be found in only a small number of secondary schools, the idea is clearly spreading upward from the primary level (formerly grades 1, 2, and 3) where it still enjoys its greatest support. In fact, figures from the U.S. Office of Education and the National Education Association suggest a rapidly accelerating trend.

In a sense, colleges and universities may be regarded as nongraded, since they provide for an almost unlimited range of student interests. Doctoral programs certainly have many of the characteristics associated with nongradedness, for doctoral candidates are working at their own pace on problems suited to their interests and needs.

High schools that offer advanced courses for the more capable students are creating new opportunities and problems for the colleges. Students who complete honors courses or advanced placement courses in high school are admitted to advanced standing (sophomore level, or above) in many colleges. In 1963–64, for example, over 10 percent of the entering class of about twelve hundred men at Harvard College were accorded full sophomore standing because their secondary schools had prepared them adequately in the regular freshman subjects; 520 others were accorded advanced placement in at least one subject. The effect of such preparation is to shorten in length, or to increase in depth, the college experience of well-qualified students and of their graduate-school experience as well.

This trend has prompted speculation on the roles that high schools and colleges will be playing in the future. Robert Maynard Hutchins, for example, has suggested that the colleges as presently organized and operated may be becoming obsolete, with some of their former functions now being served by secondary schools and others by universities.

Over the years, colleges have experimented with programs that bear a striking resemblance to those of the nongraded school. Recently, stimulated by the trend toward nongradedness in the high schools and by their own growing awareness of student needs and potentialities, many colleges have stepped up the pace of such experimentation. In 1963 and 1964, for example, the School of Engineering and Applied Science of George Washington University introduced a new plan that abolished the traditional classifications of freshman, sophomore, junior, and senior. Instead, students were grouped according to level of accomplishment: introductory, intermediate, or advanced. Under this plan each student sets his own goals and standards (with the help of a faculty adviser) and moves forward at whatever rate he is capable of. Beginning students are required to take placement examinations, and remedial work is prescribed in areas where they prove deficient. There are no formal course requirements at either the introductory or the intermediate level, and advancement from one level to the next is based on comprehensive evaluation examinations. At the advanced level, students concentrate in a particular area of engineering or applied science; here specific courses are required, although individual variations are possible. The advanced program consists of approximately thirty-five semester hours; the intermediate program, about thirty-five; and the introductory program, seventy.

Another instance of increased efforts to increase individualization and flexibility at the college level is the new program of experimental courses announced by Bucknell University. Beginning in the fall of 1966, students in these courses were able to progress at their own speed. They receive up to twelve credits per semester, depending on how far they have progressed, instead of the usual three credits. At the outset, the program included courses in biology, psychology, and philosophy; if it proves successful, the plan will be extended to other subjects.

PROBLEMS, CAUTIONS, AND DISADVANTAGES

As we have noted, research on the nongraded school has not yet produced a significant body of reliable evidence. A few studies have given support to the argument that nongrading improves the mental health of both teachers and pupils. Children at the extremes of the ability continuum appear to profit academically from the nongraded arrangement, parent attitudes are said to improve, and teachers seem to become more aware of individual pupil needs. These and other positive statements have received some support from the reports released to date.

What about the other side of the story? What are some of the seeming disadvantages of the nongraded arrangement? The most persistent, and probably the most valid, complaint is that the majority of so-called nongraded classes are imperfect or invalid examples of the theoretical ideal. Obviously, this is scarcely a complaint against nongrading itself. Nevertheless, a serious problem arises when those who are engaged in developing and evaluating the nongraded arrangement fail to provide a working model and to provide practical clues for those who wish to develop the idea on their own.

Although there is no literature that can be called genuinely "anti-nongraded," several authors have pointed out some of the problems and questions that are being raised. Stuart Dean has listed ten reasons why some observers do not consider the nongraded school desirable. Here is his list,[8] together with the present author's comments:

ALLEGATION	COMMENT
1. Nongradedness leads to soft pedagogy; it lacks fixed standards and requirements.	1. This is probably true in the early stages, but as we grow more skillful in curriculum development, appropriate standards for each type of child are likely to emerge. Nongradedness may, indeed, lead us *away* from soft pedagogy by enabling all youngsters to master what they study.

8. Adapted from Stuart E. Dean, "The Nongraded School: Is There Magic in It?" *School Life*, 47 (December 1964), pp. 22–23.

ALLEGATION	COMMENT
2. It places an impossible burden on the teacher.	2. Quite true, especially if we persist in having self-contained classrooms! The burden will lift as we find ways of sharing teaching responsibilities.
3. It replaces grade requirements by reading levels.	3. Only in the primitive stages and where nongrading is not well understood.
4. It results in a lack of information on pupil progress to parents.	4. Only when the teachers are lazy, foolish, or incompetent in their reporting.
5. It is difficult to put into practice, because teachers are inadequately and insufficiently prepared.	5. True. Therefore, let's start a revolution in teacher education!
6. It does not have minimal standards for all children.	6. It is better to have standards for *each child,* is it not?
7. Its curriculum sequence tends to lack specificity and order.	7. Again, if true it may be just as well! What we need, it must be admitted, is a *far* more adequate curriculum. The graded curriculum is scarcely the ideal.
8. It is only an improved means to an unimproved end.	8. This sounds like double-talk, but if the end is individual fulfillment then nongradedness is a better way to get there.
9. It does not guarantee that improved teaching will result.	9. No organization provides such a guarantee. To improve teaching is a very difficult task.
10. It suffers from widespread use and even abuse of the term "nongraded."	10. Amen!

Another useful list of disadvantages is provided by Maurie Hillson.[9] Some of the items he mentions overlap items in Dean's list, but a few others are selected here in abbreviated form for comment:

ALLEGATION	COMMENT
11. There is some difficulty in aligning graded with nongraded schools (for example, a primary unit and a graded intermediate program).	11. This is true only if the graded unit continues to deal with youngsters in an inappropriate way. And even so, it is no problem for the children; the annoyance is only to the grade-minded teachers.

9. *Change and Innovation in Elementary School Organization: Selected Readings,* New York: Holt, Rinehart, and Winston, 1965, pp. 296–97.

ALLEGATION	COMMENT
12. Teachers and parents are so conditioned to the graded structure that they continue "grade-mindedness."	12. Yes, but over time this is a disease that can be cured.
13. Extensive records must be kept for each child.	13. Some teachers may regard this as a disadvantage but they are wrong!
14. Planning new methods of reporting to parents demands much time and work from the already heavily burdened faculty.	14. Very true. Administration must make better provision for supporting services (for example, substitute-teacher help) and for retraining teachers in the technology of reporting.

These fourteen alleged disadvantages of nongrading suggest some of the problems and difficulties that are likely to be encountered by schools and school systems that are contemplating reorganization.

Obviously, no staff can jump into nongraded organization without extensive preparation. Although the administrative changes that must be made are trivial in comparison with the curriculum decisions required, they must nevertheless be made with great care and with the full understanding and agreement of the staff. The success of a reorganization project demands that the teachers honestly believe in it and are convinced that it is necessary. Once this *conviction of need* has been established, most of the subsequent decisions can be reached quickly and surely. This is assuredly the most important lesson to be drawn from the pilot projects that have been launched to date.

Several of the fourteen allegations have to do with the increased clerical workload nongradedness puts on teachers, especially in reporting pupil progress. It is true that parents are unfamiliar with the forms of reporting required by a nongraded organization, but there is good reason to believe that parents can be won over to a system that eschews letter grades and tries to evaluate each child's performance against his own potential. Parents are even more likely to respond well if teachers and administrators take the time to examine the purposes of reporting, develop guidelines for assessing each child's potential and performance, create appropriate forms and procedures for communicating with parents (including face-to-face meetings as well as mail-outs), and work out a practical way

of protecting the teacher's time during the weeks when reports are
being prepared and presented.

Although we cannot discuss the reporting problem in detail, we
must mention that a virtual crisis is arising in the schools on this
matter. The scarcity of openings in the more highly regarded colleges and growing demands for college training within the population have persuaded an alarming number of parents that their children's chances of getting into college are closely related to success
in the high-school race for high marks and other honors. In turn,
the secondary schools have intensified the pressures on students by
fostering a very mark-conscious atmosphere. These pressures are
developing in the junior high schools and in some communities
they extend all the way down to the nursery schools.

Now, not all these pressures are bad, and the higher-caliber
college-preparatory programs now available to youngsters in the
secondary schools are in many ways commendable. However, the
difficulties of controlling these pressures, both in the school and in
the home, have assumed monstrous proportions in the minds of
many teachers, guidance counselors, and parents. Cheating scan-
dals, increases in the number of psychological referrals, vandalism,
and other forms of pupil rebellion, along with a growing tendency
among youngsters to perceive their school work as a contest for
symbolic rewards rather than as an intrinsically valuable experience, are some of the fruits of the situation that has resulted. De-
plorable as this situation is in the secondary schools, its intrusion
upon the lives of younger, less experienced children in the elementary schools looms as a national disaster.

The procedures used by teachers in reacting to and evaluating
the school performance of children can worsen or improve this
situation, and more skillful work by teachers could help prevent
the predicted disaster. Given a more accurate description of the
child's academic potential, a clearer picture of the ways in which
that potential is being realized or wasted, a better understanding
of what the teachers are trying to do in evoking desired responses
from the child, and appropriate advice on what might be done (or
avoided) in the home to encourage the child, parents would almost
certainly be better equipped to deal with their child and help him
develop realistic plans. Given teachers who have really taken the
trouble to study him and his needs in the ways mentioned, the
child would almost certainly enjoy a more profitable and appropriate school experience than now seems to be typical.

Moreover, the child would be less likely to crack under the pressures of the college-entrance problem because (1) he would not be competing in classes beyond his depth, (2) he would be less concerned about his marks as such and more concerned about learning, and (3) both he and his parents would have learned to focus their attention less on his rank in class and more on whether or not the effort he exerted and the results he achieved were commensurate with the "known possible."

This is not to say that rank in class is always unimportant or that one student should not be compared with others. Obviously, the world is competitive, and it would be naive to pretend otherwise. However, competition-with-self (to oversimplify the concept) is a far more important aspect even of life outside the school than is one's apparent position in the pecking order of one's own neighborhood, or on the job, or in the culture at large. A man must *first* know whether he is doing the best he can, and only incidentally does it matter whether others do better or worse. If this general argument makes sense, as indeed it must to the humane philosopher, then it follows that in the schools we should spend more of our energy in examining the child's performance in terms of his estimated power and less in calling attention to all the pecking-order questions that parents have been conditioned to ask over a hundred and twenty-five years of experience with graded schools.

The essential purposes and the general components of a good reporting system have been described elsewhere,[10] but neither an adequate technology nor a sense of the urgent need for improved reporting has yet been attained. In the past seven or eight years almost no research has been done in this field, and the number of doctoral studies and other research programs on reporting has been small. Despite all the exciting implications of other innovations and changes in the schools, the technology of reporting has been almost totally neglected. This situation must change in the face of increasingly urgent problems. Indeed, the future of the nongraded school depends in large measure on the success of parent-teacher communications.

Another alleged disadvantage of nongradedness (number 11, above) is that adjoining units within a school system sometimes fail to coordinate or "articulate" their programs. The nongraded pri-

---

10. See "Reporting Pupil Progress in the Nongraded School," in Goodlad and Anderson, *op. cit.*, pp. 102–41.

mary program loses some of its value and momentum when pupils move "up" to the rigid world of a literally graded fourth grade. Often the nongraded elementary school (K–6, in conventional terminology) abuts an unsympathetic and rigidly graded junior high school. Or the nongraded junior high school may confront a rigid senior high. A problem—though it is usually only a temporary one —always arises when pupils transfer from a strictly graded school to a nongraded school or from a nongraded school to a graded school.

Experience with such transfer problems suggests, however, that they are rarely serious, though they always create some measure of frustration and confusion. Most of the time, the simple fact that a family has uprooted itself and has entered into a new and unfamiliar world, the school included, is the principal source of difficulty. Usually it takes the new school only a short while to find out where the child belongs and get him back on the right track. The child who transfers from a graded school into a nongraded school is probably the more fortunate, but the child who spends even a year or two in a nongraded school is better off than he would have been if he had been in a graded atmosphere all along. At the very least, he will have developed a more realistic view of himself and his potential.

Fortunately, where some of the local units within a school system are graded and some are nongraded it is usually the lower unit that is nongraded. It is far better to postpone the child's adjustment to the graded school until he has achieved some level of maturity than it is to expose him to gradedness all the way. If the lower, nongraded unit has done its job well, and if there is at least a degree of rapport between adjacent units, it is unlikely that children will be suddenly faced with intolerable conditions.

It is no longer defensible to operate schools with rigidly defined grade-level expectancy standards. As we mentioned in chapter three, parallel and overlapping school units are needed, each capable of providing for a wide range of pupil needs and each reproducing in a slightly different context some of the services usually found in the lower or higher units, or both. For example:

1. Above-average kindergarten pupils should be able to enjoy some of the academic experiences that are usually associated with the "first grade" or even higher grades.

2. Children in the primary unit (grades 1–2–3) should, at the lower extreme, have continued exposure to kindergarten-type experiences and, at the upper extreme, exposure to academic experiences that are usually associated with the "fourth grade" and beyond.

3. Intermediate-unit pupils (grades 4–5–6), similarly, should have access both to primary-level and junior-high-school experiences.

4. The junior high or middle school should provide appropriate elementary level and senior-high experiences for its pupils.

5. The senior high, similarly, should deal gracefully and skillfully with older pupils whose attainments are in some respects at the junior-high (or even the elementary) level, while offering advanced-placement and other college-level courses to superior students.

The placement of children in teams or classes, whether on a permanent basis or for specific limited reasons, is usually based not only on academic standing but also on social and physical considerations. Sometimes an older child who is working below the normal or typical level of his age-mates [11] will actually be more comfortable in the company of notably younger children whose achievements, temperament, and interests may more nearly coincide with his own. Conversely, younger children of unusual academic competence may also be quite mature socially and physically, in which event they can be very comfortable in classes comprised of notably older pupils. Often, however, children who are academically ahead of or behind their age-mates are better kept with those age-mates (except perhaps for a few hours per day) because of social, physical, emotional, and other needs that they share with the age group. Therefore, school administrators must be prepared to make many different kinds of grouping arrangements in the schools, in accordance with what is deemed best for the total development of each child.

In summary, many of the seeming disadvantages of the nongraded school exist only because teachers and school officials have not yet developed the sophistication and flexibility that nongradedness demands. Only the curriculum-revision problems associated with nongradedness are of long-range importance and genuine severity. It may be argued, however, that nongradedness does not

---

11. The term *age-mates* as used here implies a span of several years.

cause these problems; it merely aggravates them. Since major curriculum reform is an urgent national goal, and since efforts at nongrading illuminate the need for curriculum reforms, the nongraded school may well prove to be the trigger for a much-needed and massive effort.

SUMMARY

All the following statements would be true of a full-fledged nongraded school.

1. Suitable provision is being made in all aspects of the curriculum for each unique child by such means as (a) flexible grouping and subgrouping of pupils, (b) an adaptable, flexible curriculum, (c) a great range of materials and instructional approaches.

2. The successive learning experiences of each pupil are pertinent and appropriate to his needs.

3. Each child is constantly under just the right amount of pressure. Slow learners are not subjected to too much pressure, as they are in the graded school, nor are talented learners exposed to too little.

4. Success, with appropriate rewards, is assured for all kinds of learners so long as they attend to their tasks with reasonable diligence and effort. Such success spurs the child to a conviction of his own worth and to further achievement. (a) Pupils experience occasional failure and frustration, but not nearly so much as the below-average child faces in the graded school. (b) If overconfidence and complacency occasionally arise, the teachers have not succeeded in adjusting the program to each child's capacities.

5. Grade labels and the related machinery of promotion-and-failure are nonexistent.

6. The reporting system reflects the conviction that each child is a unique individual. There are no report cards with A's and F's.

7. The teachers show sophistication in their curriculum-planning, evaluation, and record keeping.

8. For certain purposes, pupils enjoy regular social and intellectual contacts with other pupils of like mind and talent and, for other purposes, with pupils of different minds and talents.

9. The school's horizontal organization pattern allows for flexibility in grouping pupils and in utilizing the school's resources. It is *possible* to have a nongraded, self-contained classroom pattern, for example, although it is also possible to have a more flexible

horizontal arrangement such as the Dual Progress Plan, informal cooperative teaching, or full-fledged team teaching, in combination with the nongraded arrangement. The author is, of course, deeply committed to the latter (team teaching and nongradedness) as the combination much to be preferred.

Suggestions for Class Discussion and Further Investigation

1. Several large cities have shifted to nongraded schools in recent years, sometimes before the staff or the parents were properly prepared. Goodlad has commented that unless two to four years of painstaking preparation precede such a reorganization, the result may be disastrous. Discuss some of the reasons for Goodlad's warning and list some of the preparatory steps that must be taken.
2. Alexander Frazier's comment about rescuing nongradedness (see p. 51), was based in large measure on the fact that most pilot programs have merely changed to a "reading levels" plan. Visit a presumably nongraded school or read what its spokesmen have to say and try to determine whether or not bona fide nongradedness is being developed.
3. Talk with some teachers and teachers-in-training and ask them to define the nongraded school. What errors or misconceptions do you most frequently encounter? Why do you suppose these misconceptions exist? What could be done to correct them?
4. What practical problems does the concept of multiaged, heterogeneous groupings pose for the teacher? How can some of these problems be solved?
5. To what extent have either the evils of gradedness or the advantages of nongradedness as they have been defined in this chapter affected you in your own school experience? Has your experience colored your reactions to the arguments presented in this chapter?
6. By now you are probably so habituated to conventional report cards that our arguments in opposition to A–B–C–D–E–F reporting may seem extreme to you. Talk with children and parents to see whether such reporting can in fact be defended. How much information do they really obtain from such reports? What are the value and the effect of this information?

Suggestions for Further Reading

The volumes by Goodlad and Anderson, Brown, Stoddard, and Hillson that have been mentioned in this chapter constitute the major literature on the nongraded school at the present time. An extensive periodical literature has come into existence, however, and one of the volumes of the National Education Association's Project on Instruction, John Goodlad's *Planning and Organizing for Teaching,* Washington, D.C.: NEA, 1963, is of major importance.

Prospective secondary-school teachers in particular will be interested in a description of the independent study program at Melbourne High School that appears in an article by Janet Whitmire, Coordinator of Independent Study in that school, in *Phi Delta Kappan,* 47 (September 1965), pp. 43–46.

Chapter Five

Innovations in Organization: Theory and Practice in Team Teaching

THE EMERGENCE OF TEAM TEACHING

One of the most interesting and potentially significant developments in American education was the meteoric rise during the late 1950's of an organizational structure known as *team teaching*. Although the term did not appear in the *Education Index* prior to the 1957–59 volume, team teaching suddenly became a topic of sometimes violent and frequently optimistic conversation. The controversy reached a crescendo early in the 1960's. By the mid-1960's, both the historical background and the long-range usefulness of team teaching were being discussed with more scholarly objectivity, and it was becoming increasingly apparent that the concepts and procedures associated with team teaching had already wrought fundamental changes in the teaching profession.

It is almost impossible to trace even the recent history of team teaching, much less its historical antecedents. Cooperative endeavor has been by no means foreign to the experience of teachers over the past hundred years or so, and we can trace virtually all the essential characteristics of modern team organization to practices and events in both this century and the last. These events led eventually to what seemed like a revolutionary outburst from about 1955 to 1959. The word "evolutionary," however, is more representative of what actually happened.

By 1955, when several dramatic proposals concerning experimental team teaching were poised on the launching pad, American education had already entered a period of major reform. The nongraded elementary school, after a dozen or more years of trial development, had emerged as a definite alternative to conventional graded structure, and both the periodical literature and the conference programs of national organizations had begun to reflect a

71

growing interest in the nongraded movement. Educational television had emerged from the crude experimental stage, and a surge of interest had arisen in other audio-visual aids to instruction. The nation had been electrified by announcements stemming from two pioneer projects in the use of nonprofessional assistants to teachers (in Bay City, Michigan, and in the Yale-Fairfield study), and there ensued lively discussions of what teaching is and what it is not. At the same time, energetic discussion of "merit rating" was pumping smoke into meeting rooms. B. F. Skinner's work with teaching machines and programmed instruction had touched off a minor revolution in the related field of program planning and presentational technology. Criticisms of public education by writers and scholars outside the public-school establishment, as well as attacks by Rudolf Flesch and others, led to an unprecedented display of public interest in the school enterprise. This interest was later inflamed by the Russian successes in spacemanship.

More significantly, by 1955 some of the major curriculum-development projects had been launched, especially in the sciences and mathematics, with the assistance of famed university professors in the various scholarly disciplines; very shortly, these projects would make available to public-school teachers new resources and new opportunities for professional study and training. Also prominent in 1955 was the problem of the so-called gifted child, who became the object of lively concern in the literature. This concern led swiftly to a renewed interest in the more general problem of pupil grouping practices.

The years 1955–57 were a time of sharply increased collaboration between public-school systems and the colleges and universities engaged in teacher education. The postwar population boom had created an urgent shortage of qualified teachers, and many of the teacher-training programs that emerged in response to the demand called for schools and colleges to share the training responsibility. Of particular interest was the internship plan that Harvard University launched in the summer of 1955: one of its major components, the Harvard-Newton Summer Program, called for four or five apprentices to serve simultaneously under a gifted master teacher. Harvard-Newton revealed both the capacity of children for multiple relationships with adults and the advantages of cooperative-collaborative teaching arrangements. Documents prepared at Harvard under Dean Francis Keppel's leadership during 1955 and 1956, which led eventually to the Teaching Teams Project in Lexington, Massachusetts (1957–64),[1] were strongly influenced by insights gained in the Harvard-Newton Program.

Many other influences were at work in the background, not only at Harvard but in dozens of places where conventional patterns of staff organization were being questioned. Francis S. Chase of the University of Chicago, for example, had in 1953 published an article [2] pointing out that in a time when responsible and intelligent teachers are hard to find, it is necessary to use the best teachers more wisely. He called for teaching teams chaired by exceptional teachers, with teacher aides to perform clerical and nonprofessional duties. Chase predicted that such an arrangement would allow for maximal use of the available talent, provide guidance for young and inexperienced teachers, and in particular provide more attractive salaries and a more responsible role for superior teachers. Chase's statement stands as one of the real landmarks in the current school reorganization movement.

Another educator who has made a powerful contribution to this movement is J. Lloyd Trump. Trump served as Director of the Commission on the Experimental Study of the Utilization of the Staff in the Secondary School, a group supported by a grant from the Fund for the Advancement of Education. The members of this group were appointed by the National Association of Secondary-School Principals. This commission began its work in 1956 with a nationwide search for ideas and research designs on such critical problems as curriculum development, teaching methods, space arrangements, and staff utilization. Team teaching and variants thereof were subsequently explored in more than a hundred secondary schools throughout the country, and these projects promoted the first substantial literature in the field.[3]

Other examples of experimentation with team organization, all of which contributed to the rapidly growing literature, were the Norwalk Plan developed by Superintendent Harry Becker in Norwalk, Connecticut; the Wisconsin School Improvement Program, under the leadership of John Guy Fowlkes and his colleague Philip Lambert; the Claremont Graduate School teaching team program developed in California by Harris Taylor and his associates; and

---

1. This author served as Director of the Lexington Project.
2. "More and Better Teachers," *Saturday Review* (September 12, 1953), pp. 16–17.
3. In addition to Trump's published writings, see the January issues, 1958 through 1962, and also the May 1963 issue of *The Bulletin of the National Association of Secondary School Principals.*

the Englewood School program in Sarasota County, Florida, in which the author and John I. Goodlad helped to develop team teaching in the context of a nongraded elementary school.

Although this list does not include all the pioneer projects that deserve to be included when the early history of team teaching is eventually written, it suggests the fairly broad geographical base and the great diversity of the movement even at the outset. It also confirms the fact that no one person or organization actually founded the movement, and it supports the general argument that conditions propitious for the overturning of long-established conventional arrangements had already come into being throughout the country by 1955–59.

All these men and projects, for example, were undoubtedly influenced by and sensitive to the growing disenchantment with the rigid vertical structure of graded schools. Many of the same forces that led to the erosion of graded practices were also taking their toll of the self-contained classroom and other practices that required teachers to operate in relative isolation from one another.

For at least a quarter of a century, teachers had been engaging in a variety of efforts at formal or informal collaboration. These efforts included the combining of classes for specific purposes, the exchange of functions among teachers with different interests and strengths, various means of subdividing the total work load, and the pooling of classes prior to temporary regrouping for some purpose (for example, the teaching of reading in an elementary school or the establishment of project committees in high-school science). Informal hierarchical organization, though voluntary, has existed in the past in many schools. Especially in larger high schools and in those with core programs, teachers in the same division or department have often functioned much in the manner of teams. An example that comes immediately to mind, of course, is in athletics, where several coaches serve together under a head coach.

A parallel may also be found in the training program of the armed forces, where many of the practices later associated with team teaching were developed during the Second World War. Many of the men who later became involved in the educational reform movement took part in these training programs either as instructors or as trainees.

Cooperative teaching practices, of course, have long been familiar in nursery school teaching and kindergarten programs. At the college level and in medical education, cooperative research and cooperative teaching were common before the 1950's. Often several instructors worked together in conducting large courses and even seminars. The phrase "teaching teams" was used as early as 1941 to describe a collaborative teaching enterprise at Troy State Teachers College in Alabama.

The staff at Troy, in an attempt to reconstruct its program of teacher education, set up a new plan for the freshman entering in 1940–41. "A definite effort was made to provide for a better integration of subject matter by organizing the instructional staff in teaching teams which would cut across subject interests, and by setting up large-unit courses." [4] Each of the core or comprehensive courses was managed by a staff team made up of from two to four members, each representing a different field of specialization. Other members of the college staff—for example, the college nurse, physician, dietician, and dean of women—were designated as special resource members. Each team had a chairman who was responsible for organizing the team and arranging for the effective use of the resource people. "This would naturally involve planning conferences of the team staff at intervals in order that the contributions of team members would be used more effectively." [5]

Stover's descriptions of the class schedule, the combination-class and large-unit undertakings, the flexible interest groupings, and other operational details suggest that the team-teaching arrangement in Troy was very similar to more recent plans. There are also references to team counseling and to various forms of cooperative interaction among staff members.

ANTECEDENTS OF THE CURRENT TEAM-TEACHING MOVEMENT

Earlier, when we spoke of graded practices, we used the term "erosion." As that word implies, conventional patterns of horizontal organization and staff utilization gave way very slowly. There were, however, certain dramatic episodes and "giant steps" along the way, as efforts were made to provide more appropriate and indi-

---

4. G. Franklin Stover, "The Freshman Program in General Education for 1940–41," Troy State Teachers College *Bulletin*, 28 (October 1941), p. 8.
5. *Ibid.*, p. 10.

vidualized instruction for pupils or to make more efficient use of human and material resources. Most of these efforts sprang from a desire for more flexibility and for operational solutions to problems that had been uncovered by studies of child development and learning theory. (Some of these were mentioned in the preceding chapter.) A few, such as the monitorial system developed by Andrew Bell and Joseph Lancaster during the early nineteenth century, are now of interest primarily because they illuminate the raw, primitive conditions under which England and America were forced to develop their public school systems and, only in very small part, because of their relevance to current theories about staff utilization. Later in the nineteenth century and early in the twentieth, a number of others represented serious efforts to develop theoretically desirable arrangements, such as the use of assistant teachers to make possible more individualized instruction. Much more recently, such plans have been linked to some of the newer plans for teacher education.

In a plan that developed in 1898 more or less accidentally as a temporary means of coping with overcrowded classes, John Kennedy, superintendent of the schools in Batavia, New York, proposed that two teachers be assigned to the same classroom, one to handle group recitations and the other to work with individual pupils. The Batavia Plan was picked up and developed by other school systems, but it survived for only about thirty years. It gave way eventually to a strong trend toward smaller class sizes.

One of the most famous and productive of the superintendents who shaped American education around the turn of the century was Preston W. Search. A plan introduced by Search in Pueblo, Colorado, in 1880 eliminated the concept of nonpromotion, emphasized individual work and individual progress, and called for the use of assistant teachers. A remarkable little book by Search, *An Ideal School: or, Looking Forward*, published in 1901, dared to propose arrangements that bear an astonishing resemblance to certain "new ideas" in our own time. For example, Search proposed to free teachers from routine functions (an idea that went unused about fifty years, until the Bay City and Yale-Fairfield projects came along), to join teachers in a federation for planning purposes, to build teacher-training functions into the very fabric of the school itself, to pay adequate, "discriminative" salaries, and to give teachers an opportunity to observe practices in the better schools, "or better still, by association in the same school with co-workers who represent, in their selection, the best personnel and the best methods." [6]

From 1896 to 1903, John Dewey and his associates operated the Laboratory School of the University of Chicago. American education will forever profit from some of the ideas underlying that noble experiment. Dewey's work was in large measure a rebellion against rigid graded structures (as, indeed, were most of the other reform movements), but it may surprise the present-day educator to learn that Dewey was among the first to argue for team teaching! Dewey's phrase was "cooperative social organization," and it was his intention that intellectual association and exchange should be a major factor in the lives of pupils and teachers alike. As Dewey's school grew larger, it came to have a departmental organization. Dewey regarded the word "departmental" as unfortunate, however:

> It suggests a kind of compartmentalizing and isolation of forms of work that should be integrated with one another. But experience has convinced me that there cannot be all-around development of either teachers or pupils without something for which the only available word is departmental teaching, though I should prefer to speak of lines of activity carried on by persons with special aptitude, interest, and skill in them. It is the absence of cooperative intellectual relations among teachers that causes the present belief that young children must be taught everything by one teacher, and that leads to so-called departmental teaching being strictly compartmental with older ones. [7]

In later sections of the Mayhew and Edwards book there are references to the extraordinary amount and quality of interaction and discussion Dewey sought to promote, along with comments highly critical of the arrangement that came to be known and for a time was almost revered as the self-contained classroom.

Of both historical and current importance is the work of Dr. Maria Montessori, an Italian physician whose unique program for early childhood education had a notable impact on American schools from 1911 to 1952 and whose ideas are currently enjoying a revival of interest. Montessori anticipated the idea of team teaching and, in her discussion of pre-adolescents, indicated the need for professional competency well beyond that possessed by ordinary teachers. She advocated that children be grouped in such a

6. New York: Appleton and Co., International Education Series, 1901, pp. 305–06.
7. Quoted in Katherine C. Mayhew and Anna C. Edwards, *The Dewey School: The Laboratory School of the University of Chicago, 1896–1903*, New York: Appleton-Century, 1936, pp. 371–72.

way that large groups of children working independently could be alternated with smaller groups engaged in group lessons and discussion.

Every student of American education is (or should be) familiar with William A. Wirt's Platoon School Plan, Carleton Washburne's Winnetka Plan, and Helen Parkhurst's Dalton Plan. Wirt's plan, which he developed in Indiana around 1900, is sometimes known as the work-study-play school, because it aimed to ensure proportionate emphasis on each of these three major aspects of the child's life. It called for the division of the pupils into two platoons. Classes were scheduled so that half of the time was devoted to academic subjects in homerooms and the other half was spent in the activities requiring special facilities or laboratories: manual arts, home economics, nature study, art, music, physical education, auditorium experiences, and library work.

The Winnetka Plan (dating to 1919), much of which derives from the earlier work (dating from 1912) of President Frederic Burk in the San Francisco State College training school, called for the division of the curriculum into two parts. The "common essentials" —that is, the basic subjects that all children must master—occupied half of each day, with the pupil working independently on unit lessons until he felt ready to take the mastery test. Group and creative activities (for example, literature, music, art, handiwork, playground activities) occupied the other half of the day. Here there were no specific standards for the children to meet. Homeroom placement of the children was based on age and social maturity, and children could be moved rather easily from one group to another as their individual progress warranted. The Winnetka Plan is actually an antecedent of the present-day nongraded school, and it was probably the first major example of what is now called programmed instruction. It is also notable for its direct and indirect contributions to the current team-teaching movement, especially in respect to cooperative staff planning and program development. Its story, too, is a remarkable illustration of what can happen when a professional staff strives, as did Carleton Washburne and his associates, to develop the competencies shown in the diagram on page 19.[8]

---

8. The full story of the famous Winnetka school system (1919 to 1963) is now available in a highly recommended volume: Carleton W. Washburne and Sidney P. Marland, Jr., *Winnetka: The History and Significance of an Educational Experiment*, Englewood Cliffs, N.J.: Prentice-Hall, 1963.

The Dalton Plan, used mostly from grade 4 through high school, was first introduced in 1919 in a school for crippled children; in 1920 it was adopted by a high school in Dalton, Massachusetts. Its major emphasis was on group life rather than on the curriculum itself. The academic subjects were taught largely on an individual basis, with each subject laid out in a series of related jobs known as "contracts," each of which required about a month's work. The pupil could complete each contract at his own speed, but he was required to maintain an even pace across all subject lines lest he neglect some areas in favor of others. The nonacademic subjects were taught by class or group methods, and the classes consisted of multiaged groups on a nongraded basis. The Dalton Plan called for specialist teachers, each teaching in a room specially equipped for his subject. In the larger schools, the pupils were grouped in multiaged divisions of 200 to 250 students.

These three plans are closely related to Stoddard's Dual Progress Plan in several important respects. Since all three have survived, though in greatly modified form, up to the present time, we can observe how they both influenced and were influenced by the current educational reform movements.

A pioneer whose work bears a more direct relationship to the modern pattern of team teaching than any of the other innovators mentioned so far was James F. Hosic. Hosic's scheme, developed in the early 1930's, was known as the Cooperative Group Plan. Its main feature was the organization of the teaching staff into small cooperative groups of three to six teachers, one of whom served as chairman. Specialization in teaching was another salient feature, and each group of teachers (on either the primary or the intermediate level) worked with the same pupils for a three-year period. Apparently the plan was adopted for a time in some New York City schools, but Henry J. Otto (whose brief discussion of the plan seems to be the only record available [9]) reports that no published evaluations have ever appeared and that there are no data on how widely it was used. Shaplin regards the Cooperative Group Plan as an outstanding and well-conceived example of what is now called team teaching and suggests that it disappeared because it was ahead of its time. [10]

---

9. *Elementary School Organization and Administration,* 3rd ed., New York: Appleton-Century-Crofts, 1954, pp. 148–51.
10. Judson T. Shaplin, "Antecedents of Team Teaching," Shaplin and Henry F. Olds, Jr., eds., *Team Teaching,* New York: Harper and Row, 1964, p. 50.

In summary, the concepts and procedures embodied in such current phrases as team teaching and nongraded school organization owe their existence and much of their vitality to hundreds if not thousands of advances, both in Europe and America, toward the goal of truly individualized instruction. Many of these were probably little known even in their own day, but fortunately a few of them have left us a record to admire.

Any attempt to define team teaching as a strictly new idea that sprang from the head of some modern Zeus reveals a lack of historical perspective. Our debt to the giants of the past and to some who still walk and work among us is truly incalculable.

TEAM TEACHING DEFINED

Conventional Alternatives. Team teaching is a pattern of horizontal school organization [11] that has emerged as an alternative to the self-contained elementary-school classroom and the departmentalized arrangements found in most secondary schools and some elementary schools. In a sense, it embodies the advantages generally ascribed to those two conventional patterns but seeks to avoid certain of their disadvantages.

Among the alleged advantages of the self-contained classroom are the following:

1. Children identify themselves with a small, stable group of fellow students and gain security and satisfaction thereby.

2. Since children need to adjust to the personality and teaching style of only one adult, confusion and conflict are reduced.

3. The personal, social, and emotional well-being of each child is promoted, because one teacher who sees him under a wide range of circumstances is constantly attentive to his needs and development.

4. The total educational experience of the child has an assured unity, because its components are managed and planned by a single teacher capable of fitting all the parts together.

5. The teacher enjoys a high degree of flexibility in the use of class time through the school day.

6. Children identify with and accept responsibility for the classroom environment which is their "home."

---

11. That is, a way of "packaging" the pupils and the teachers in a school at any given moment in time. See chapter three, page 30.

Some of the disadvantages that are sometimes ascribed to the self-contained classroom are these:

1. It is impossible, as knowledge increases and the curriculum becomes more complicated, for any one teacher to know enough about all the content areas, to maintain a genuine interest in them, and to communicate this interest in appropriate ways to children.

2. It is unlikely that any one teacher's personality and teaching style will be appropriate for *all* the twenty-five to thirty children who may be assigned to him.

3. Continuous confinement to a single, restricted physical environment over ten months will prove monotonous and unstimulating to children.

4. Teachers inevitably suffer various cultural biases or prejudices that make it potentially dangerous to entrust to any *one* of them, over an extended period of time, the complete responsibility for transmission of the culture and the performance of guidance functions.

5. The teacher's work-a-day responsibilities are continuous and unbroken except for those occasional interruptions when specialist teachers in music, art, and physical education take over the class.

6. Since the teacher works in private, it is possible for him to "bluff" his way along.

In a departmentalized organization each teacher is assigned to a particular teaching area (for example, mathematics); consequently, pupils encounter several different teachers in the course of the day. This arrangement is generally acknowledged to have the following advantages:

1. Since each teacher has an avowed preference for the subject he teaches and has had extensive education in that field (through his college major and his professional methods courses), his performance is likely to be highly competent.

2. The subgrouping of pupils in the various disciplines is flexible, because the groups can be drawn from a large population.

3. Classrooms reserved for specific teaching functions can be provided with equipment and furnishings specifically suited to those functions (science laboratories, for example).

On the other hand, many believe that departmental organization has two disadvantages:

1. Since teachers and departments tend to function in isolation, there is poor integration of the overall curriculum experience of each pupil.

2. Because there is a lack of communication among the several teachers who deal with each pupil, his overall guidance needs are rarely a matter of joint concern.

Until cooperative teaching patterns appeared as an alternative to these two conventional patterns, the overwhelming majority of administrators and teachers accepted with few reservations the advantages ascribed to the self-contained classroom. Only a handful of elementary schools made any deliberate use of departmental organization. The others, of course, cheerfully tolerated the intervention of various specialists (for example, music, art, physical education, library, and remedial reading), and there was a great deal of informal collaboration among the presumably self-contained teachers. Nearly all the "experts" in elementary education were convinced that the self-contained classroom was an ideal arrangement. Understandably, the typical reaction of the profession to the pilot team-teaching projects between 1955 and about 1959 was one of outrage and disbelief.

It is, of course, far too early for us to assess the ultimate value of self-containment, departmentalization, or team teaching, but we can at least describe their probable strengths and weaknesses. On the whole, the evidence tends to confirm the alleged advantages and disadvantages of departmentalization listed above. The alleged advantages of the self-contained classroom are difficult to prove, however, and its disadvantages are becoming increasingly evident.

As a matter of fact, a great deal of what we once thought we knew about the bases of pupil security, about the optimum teacher-pupil relationship, about children's emotional and personal needs, about the size and the composition of classes (and schools), about pupil grouping for this purpose and that, and about curriculum planning has been subjected to careful reexamination as a result of the iconoclastic development of team teaching. Some rather surprising discoveries have been made; and although the data are by no means complete, we can at least say that team teaching (as we shall define it in a moment) now stands confirmed as a legitimate and probably superior alternative to the self-contained arrangement that was once held sacred as the *sine qua non* of elementary education.

Types of Cooperative Teaching. There are almost as many definitions of team teaching as there are people writing about it. (In many respects, the more generic term "cooperative teaching" is preferable.) The tendency has been to use the term team teaching so broadly that it serves as a label for fairly conventional and loosely organized arrangements as well as for more elaborate and formalized structures.

Throughout this book, we use the terms cooperative teaching and team teaching more or less interchangeably, sometimes merely to avoid the monotonous repetition of one or the other phrase. In this section, however, we must make certain distinctions for the sake of clarity.

Team teaching is a formal type of cooperative staff organization in which a group of teachers accepts the responsibility for planning, carrying out, and evaluating an educational program, or some major portion of a program, for an aggregate of pupils. Usually there are twenty to thirty pupils for each full-time adult involved. As such, team teaching is a relatively structured form of cooperative teaching; less formalized versions are perhaps better designated by a term other than team teaching.

It is possible to view *cooperative teaching* as embracing a wide range of formal and informal patterns of cooperation and coinvolvement. Earlier in this chapter we might have mentioned, along with other historical antecedents of team teaching, such informal arrangements as the occasional combining of classes, the exchange of teaching functions ("You teach my science for me and I'll teach your music"), the pooling and interchange of pupils, [12] and joint planning by teachers with similar responsibilities.

Paul Woodring, writing in the 1964 yearbook of the National Society for the Study of Education, suggests that many projects officially described as "team teaching" might be accurately described as "team organization and planning," since the collaboration that actually takes place is often limited to planning and preparation. This was a reasonable and accurate analysis at the time of which Woodring was speaking, and it is by no means to be interpreted as a critical or unfriendly observation on his part. Teachers are on the whole very receptive to arguments favoring

---

12. As in the Joplin Plan for reading instruction, where several teachers agree to interchange pupils for the purpose of establishing homogeneous reading groups.

joint planning, and many benefits are known to accrue from this type of teamwork, whether or not teachers also cooperate in teaching and evaluation activities. Our definition of team teaching, however, embraces not only planning but the actual teaching and the subsequent evaluation as well. So we shall examine some of the patterns that include all these functions.

A marginal example in which coinvolvement in teaching and especially in evaluation is sometimes very limited is the "master-teacher plan" found in some secondary schools. Under this arrangement, a prestigious and talented master teacher is assisted by colleagues in a sequence that includes large-group lectures or demonstrations by the master teacher and follow-up discussion sections led by the other teachers. The progenitor of this arrangement is the scheme used in large universities for popular, large-enrollment courses where the senior professor delivers the lectures and junior colleagues conduct the more intimate seminars or section meetings. Although such arrangements have obvious limitations, they sometimes work out very well.

Many of the so-called team-teaching projects, especially in the secondary schools, are in effect voluntary federations of sovereign teachers—the participants have, metaphorically speaking, touched fingers without interlocking arms. The teachers in these projects often function within the fairly conventional lines of departmental structure and remain relatively independent; the quality and quantity of actual coinvolvement fluctuates in accordance with the separate moods and wishes of the participants. One way of describing this kind of arrangement would be to show several wedges of cheese, spread in a circle around a tray but slightly separated from each other:

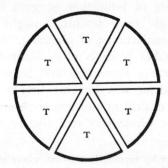

T = Teacher

A more full-fledged version of team teaching may be depicted as a cut pie whose pieces remain unseparated in the tin:

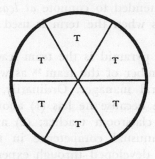

This analogy suggests that each participant in the project is closely associated with his colleagues; it implies a partial merging of sovereignties in return for the privileges of partnership. It also implies that the partners in such a team are essentially equal in terms of prestige, responsibility, and leadership functions. Often, the formalized leadership is essentially parliamentary: a designated member serves pro tem as the chairman of meetings and possibly as a representative of the group, but he has no real authority or responsibility beyond that of his colleagues. Sometimes, the chairmanship actually rotates so that everyone takes his turn and the equalitarian image is maintained.

Finally, we may depict the most formal version of team teaching by means of a pyramid:

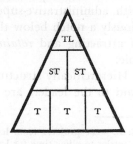

TL = Team Leader
ST = Senior Teacher (or Specialist Teacher)
T = Teacher

This picture represents the hierarchical pattern of team organization, in which there are two or more levels of prestige, responsibility, and leadership. At the base of the pyramid are the fully qualified professionals for whom the standard word "teacher" is used. It cannot be stated too strongly that the word "teacher" as used in this context is intended to connote *at least as prestigious* and respectable a role as when the term is used in the conventional American setting.

At the top of the pyramid is the team leader, who serves as a regular teaching member of the team [13] as well as the team's coordinator and general manager. Ordinarily, the team leader is selected for the role because he has (1) above-average if not superior talents as a classroom teacher; (2) a particular teaching strength (such as unusual competence in teaching elementary-school mathematics) developed through experience and advanced training; (3) unusual ability in curriculum planning, the analysis of instructional problems and procedures, the diagnosis and evaluation of pupil behavior, and other dimensions of the "hypotenuse" concept developed in chapter two; (4) the skills usually associated with group leadership, such as sound understanding of group dynamics; and (5) a willingness to carry the sometimes burdensome responsibilities associated with the leader's role.

The leadership responsibility demands more emotional, physical, and intellectual energy than the standard teaching role. Consequently, advocates of hierarchical structure contend that it should command a higher financial reward in the marketplace. Sometimes, therefore, the team leader in a hierarchically structured team is paid a supplement ($1,000, for example) above the regular salary schedule for teachers. Since this practice enables a classroom teacher in the leadership role to earn a salary that compares favorably with administrative-supervisory salaries in education (though obviously a notch below them), it is thought to heighten the chances of attracting and *retaining* high-quality candidates in a teaching role.

Hierarchically structured teams in which salary supplements are paid to the leaders are not yet very numerous, and the tradition

---

13. In some projects, team leaders may have a slightly reduced teaching load in order to allow time for leadership functions, but it is important to emphasize that the team leader is primarily a fellow teacher and only secondarily an administrative-supervisory person. This contrasts with the principalship, another leadership role, in which *only* administrative-supervisory functions are involved.

of equalitarian, uniform salary schedules is not likely to be surrendered cheerfully by the majority of teachers already in the profession. However, it seems possible that as the profession gains more experience in the selection of leaders and as a new generation of talented young people becomes aware of the additional inducements the teaching role can now offer in certain communities, the practice may grow in acceptance if not in popularity.

The hierarchical pyramid also shows an intermediate role of leadership, that of "senior teacher" or "specialist teacher." While some hierarchical teams include only two strata at the professional level (team leader and teacher), others provide for three levels of prestige and responsibility; the middle level is more that of a "master teacher" than of an administrator-supervisor. Of the five qualifications listed above for team leader, a senior teacher is ordinarily expected to possess the first three (teaching skill, a specialization, and general "hypotenuse" strength) to perhaps the same degree as a team leader; less emphasis is placed on leadership talent and the willingness to carry full responsibility. A salary supplement of perhaps half that paid to the team leader is generally provided as an incentive and as recognition of the prestige and responsibility associated with the role.

We must now mention one of the misconceptions that sometimes arise when team teaching is discussed. In a profession that is vociferously unfriendly, on the whole, to merit rating, hierarchical team structure is sometimes seen as a scheme to introduce merit rating in disguise. That accusation is unjustified. Merit rating, as the term is commonly used, implies the payment of supplements or awards to teachers who are judged to be more effective and useful in the classroom than other teachers of equivalent background and length of service who are performing the same role. In hierarchically structured team teaching higher salaries are indeed paid to the more effective and useful teachers, but these teachers are assigned to roles in which they not only continue to provide superior services to their pupils but in which they engage in the *different* and presumably more difficult tasks associated with the senior teacher and team leader roles. In other words, the qualities that merit rating seeks to reward are merely *a part* of the reason the senior teacher and team leader receive additional salary. Moreover, since the extra responsibilities of the senior teacher and team leader are evident to the teachers with whom they work, the regular teachers are less likely to feel that they have been unfairly treated than are teachers in nonteam schools whose fellow teachers receive merit supplements.

Let us summarize what we have said about informal and formal types of cooperative teaching:

TYPES OF COOPERATIVE TEACHING

Informal

Simple, voluntary collaboration without structure or assumption of permanence.	Informal team structure with voluntary membership and relative ease of withdrawal ("cheese wedges").
Division of responsibility to simplify workload or preparation.	Older teacher working with an apprentice or younger teacher (relationship temporary).
Interchange of pupils for specific grouping purposes.	
Combining of classes for specific experiences.	

Formal

Formalized team structure with leadership designated on a continuing or rotating basis; leader primarily a chairman, peer status emphasized ("pie tin").	Formalized team structure on hierarchical basis, leader in assumed permanent role and with salary supplement or equivalent remuneration ("pyramid").
Teacher or teachers assisted by teacher aide on a continuing basis.	Formalized, hierarchical structure with several levels of responsibility above that of teacher.

Essential and Desirable Characteristics. In the preceding section we defined team teaching by pointing to several kinds of informal and formal patterns calling for significant interaction and collaboration. Of the several types illustrated this author prefers the hierarchically structured pyramid with salary supplements for the leaders. It seems that economic and prestige incentives can be effective in recruiting and retaining a lively and imaginative corps of teachers. It also seems that hierarchical structure is a more realistic and effective arrangement than the pie-shaped equalitarian pattern.

However, it would be erroneous to claim that the pie (and even the cheese plate) has no place in the future scheme of things. To prefer the pyramid is not to insist on it. Judson T. Shaplin, co-editor of the most significant book [14] thus far produced in the grow-

---

14. Shaplin and Olds, eds., *op. cit.*

ing literature of team teaching, points out that any tendency to insist on hierarchical structure and role differentiation might cause the team-teaching movement to fall of its own weight, as apparently did Hosic's Cooperative Group Plan and several other highly specific plans in the past.[15] Certainly, this is a fair warning and a plausible argument; at most, we may cite hierarchical structure as a very logical and attractive arrangement but not an absolute requirement in our definition of team organization.

Among the other characteristics of team teaching listed by various authors are: (1) specialization or differentiation in teaching functions; (2) flexible subgrouping of pupils within the context of the total pupil population; (3) flexible and efficient use of the various resources within the school, including the building itself; (4) ease of incorporating part-time teachers, itinerant specialist teachers, and other personnel, including nonprofessionals, in the team's structure; (5) greater tendency to use a wider range of instructional resources and teaching technologies; (6) ease and effectiveness of incorporating and training apprentices and beginning teachers; and (7) built in opportunities for stimulating each team member's professional growth. Notice the extent to which flexibility and efficiency ("passwords" to this text mentioned in chapter one) are explicitly and implicitly ascribed to cooperative teaching in such listings as these.

Particularly impressive is the suggestion that team teaching offers an appropriate environment not only for the training and induction of newcomers to the profession, but also for the advancement of each experienced teacher's professional knowledge and skill. In chapter two we mentioned that criticism is sadly missing from the lives of most teachers. Exposure to the constructive reactions and suggestions of colleagues, within the atmosphere of a full-fledged team operation, would seem almost to guarantee continual self-examination and professional study. Seen as an instrument of the profession for keeping its members constantly active as students of their own role, team teaching therefore emerges as a development potentially equal in importance to the idea of graduate study and certainly superior to the usual ineffectual devices employed hopefully by local systems under the title "in-service training for teachers."

---

15. Judson T. Shaplin, "Cooperative Teaching: Definitions and Organizational Analysis," *The National Elementary Principal*, 44 (January 1965), p. 20.

At the preservice level, team organization is sometimes used as a setting for student teaching, even though the young teachers so trained may not necessarily contemplate eventual membership in a team as such. A few colleges, for example, organize their "master teachers" in teams to which apprentices [16] are assigned, not so much because the apprentices will gain experience as team members per se but because they will be exposed to a variety of teaching styles and to the intrateam conversations of the master teachers about teaching and curriculum planning. Other colleges have programs in which their more senior students are assigned to a team as interns with full status as participating members; the resulting experience is more nearly like that of a beginning teacher than that of a mere apprentice. In a program at the University of Wisconsin several interns are assigned to a team comprising several veteran teachers and perhaps an aide; through associations with the veteran teachers, the interns usually enter into and pass beyond the stage of beginning teacher. Harvard University has for some years assigned certain of its interns to teaching teams in Lexington, Massachusetts, and other nearby communities for a semester of full-time teaching. This and other arrangements have proved to be exceptionally powerful instruments of teacher preparation.

As in the case of hierarchical structure, the inclusion of teachers-in-training in the team's membership is a very desirable though not indispensable aspect of team teaching. Similarly, the inclusion of nonprofessionals and the extensive use of certain grouping practices or specialized technologies, or both, are desirable but not indispensable. About all that can be regarded as truly essential would be that (1) the team be so composed as to ensure the range and depth of talents necessary to the teaching tasks required; (2) these talents be deployed in whatever ways are necessary to achieve maximum efficiency and coverage; (3) the total group of pupils, rather than just subgroups, be regarded as the population for which joint responsibility is shared; and (4) the coinvolvement of the

---

16. The terms *apprentice, beginning teacher,* and *intern teacher* are sometimes used with different meanings. Here, the term *apprentice* indicates a student serving under the immediate and constant supervision of a master teacher whose class is in effect being "loaned" to the apprentice on occasion; *intern* means a person who has already served an apprenticeship or equivalent preparation and is filling a regular teaching position under somewhat less constant supervision; and *beginning teacher* means a fully trained person who, though still inexperienced, is usually expected to perform about as well as a veteran teacher.

teachers be sufficiently genuine that real flexibility is achieved and real professional growth is stimulated.

This latter point is one of the keys to understanding the nature and significance of team teaching. People are constantly asking, "What is the best form of team teaching?" Our answer, once the various possible arrangements and characteristics mentioned above have been briefly considered, would be as follows.

An "Ideal" Conception of Team Teaching. The full benefits of team organization are not likely to be reaped unless the team members are literally coinvolved (we might even say immersed) in all three phases of teaching: planning, actual work in carrying out the plan with children, and evaluating the results. Therefore, in an ideal arrangement:

1. All team members (including children, wherever possible) participate in formulating broad overall objectives for the total program.

2. All team members participate at least weekly in formulating the more immediate objectives of the program.

3. All team members have an opportunity from time to time to contribute to the specific daily planning of their colleagues, and vice versa. That is to say, Miss Jones's lesson plan for Thursday afternoon is presented, discussed, and (it is hoped) modified for the better in Tuesday's team planning session, and, in turn, Miss Jones has equivalent opportunities to examine and improve the plans of her teammates.

4. Therefore, all team members are at all times at least conversant with the specific daily plans and professional repertoires of the other team members. As a result, it would be relatively easy for any team member to step into a colleague's teaching shoes in an emergency.

5. All team members at least occasionally (that is, several times a week) carry on teaching functions in the actual presence of colleagues who are either taking some part in the same lesson or simply sitting in as interested observers.

6. All team members participate periodically (weekly, if possible) in evaluation sessions of the overall as well as the current program.

7. And finally, each team member is the beneficiary of at least one weekly conference in which episodes of his own teaching (preferably those to which one or more colleagues were witnesses) are

carefully and objectively analyzed and out of which specific suggestions and ideas for professional improvements emanate.

Since these requirements are very difficult to meet in the typical school because of the problem of time, they border on the unrealistic or unreasonable. However, unless each of the seven conditions exists to some significant degree in the life of the team, many of the advantages ascribed to team organization will be forfeited, and those who claim to be working as a team will experience a great deal of self-deception and disappointment. As we discovered in an earlier chapter, real nongrading is very difficult to achieve completely but is still a goal toward which we dare not stop striving. Similarly the ideal conditions of team teaching represent a beautiful constellation of stars at which to shoot.

While we are stargazing, we may as well take a stand on some of the optional features that are associated with an ideal plan. We have already stated our preference for hierarchical structure. A constant emphasis of this book is that nongraded vertical organization and multiage pupil membership should be combined with the team structure. Certainly we would desire a generous provision of nonprofessional assistance and the inclusion of such professional personnel, including those in preservice training, as are necessary to have a complete educational program and a sufficient quantity and quality of instruction-related resources. Obviously we would also hope to locate this ideal arrangement in an ideally designed and constructed school building.

The Composition of Teams. A teaching team may be composed of a number of teachers all of whom are trained in the same academic area (for example, mathematics or French). Generally speaking, this intradepartmental or intradisciplinary type of team prevails at the senior-high-school level. Four teachers of English, for example, may be combined into an English team; by scheduling their classes and their preparation periods in the same blocks of time, they are able to take collective responsibility for several classes of simultaneously scheduled pupils. They may also work together in the planning of programs for pupils at various ages and stages of growth within the total school.

Some senior high schools and a number of junior high schools have set up interdisciplinary teams based more or less on the familiar idea of a core curriculum in which teachers trained in two or more disciplines (for example, English and social studies) have classes scheduled at the same time. They try to coordinate the programs of the related subjects as they work with simultaneously scheduled pupils.

A variation of this idea is what has been called the school-within-a-school team. Teachers from the various subject fields work for several years with the same student body in an intimate setting reserved as the team's domain. In secondary schools, this is sometimes referred to as the House Plan. Classes of different and adjustable sizes, meeting within a flexible block or modular schedule, are possible within this arrangement. This pattern has been used in programs sponsored by the Claremont Graduate School; another well-known example is the program in Newton, Massachusetts (described in *Atlantic Monthly,* October 1964).

Ira Singer has reported that in secondary schools English, social studies, and physical education are the subjects identified with team teaching at the present time. One reason may be that these are the subjects with the heaviest enrollments, for which it is easier to set up team schedules than it is for subjects with relatively few teachers and classes to be blocked together. Cooperative *planning* is a popular arrangement in many high schools,[17] and in larger high schools examples of nearly full-fledged team teaching can be found in virtually all teaching fields. There seems to be no field in which team teaching is in fact impractical or undesirable.

More team teaching is going on in the elementary schools than in the secondary schools, however. Some of the teams, especially at the upper-elementary levels, include specialists who teach only one subject in either an intradisciplinary team or an interdisciplinary arrangement. The great majority of elementary teams are "multidisciplinary," however; their members are generalists who teach all or nearly all the standard curriculum areas of science, mathematics, social studies, and the several branches of English language instruction.

One of the reasons for the emergence of elementary-school team

17. For example, ten industrial arts teachers in Phoenix, Arizona. collaborated in the preparation of color transparencies for use with an overhead projector in a drafting course. Each teacher produced master sets for one of the units, and all teachers ended up with a complete set for the course while doing only one-tenth of the work. See William J. Anderson and Carl E. Squires, "Preparing Transparencies for Drafting," *Journal of Industrial Arts Education,* 24 (September–October 1964), pp. 36–38.

teaching is that the generalist teacher has found it increasingly harder to keep abreast of new developments as the content of the various subjects becomes more complex and as pupils grow more knowledgeable. Therefore, there has been a strong tendency to require elementary teachers-in-training to undertake an undergraduate major in a content field in addition to his "major" in elementary teaching. Similarly, most advocates of team organization have pleaded for specialization within the teams, even at the primary level. They argue that a team of, say, four teachers should include one who is a bona fide specialist in elementary-school science, another who has majored and has been trained in elementary-school mathematics, another in social studies, and another in language arts.

Significantly, however, these advocates have insisted that all four teachers teach across the board lest the team idea degenerate into mere old-fashioned departmentalization. In other words, the science specialist would handle the usual teaching functions in reading, social studies, and language as well as in his own specialty. However, as a specialist he would be expected to exert a very strong influence on the overall planning of the science curriculum and on the science teaching of his colleagues. In addition, the other team members would expect him to handle the most important and the most difficult of the problems encountered in science teaching. In this way, the advantages of having specially trained teachers would be preserved without sacrificing the other values (both for pupils and for teachers) of the team organization.

In Lexington, Massachusetts, the site of the first full-scale development of team teaching in an elementary school, a useful policy was adopted early in 1957–58: "Most of the teachers in the teams will teach most of the subjects most of the time." This policy left open the *possibility* of assigning one or two teachers to a single teaching function while preserving the general principle of anti-departmentalization. This still seems a useful and defensible policy, especially at the primary level.

As the pupils grow older, it becomes more necessary to assign well-trained specialists area by area. In the senior high school, for example, there are very advanced courses that can be taught only by specialists. In general, therefore, we might conclude that between kindergarten and the end of high school there should be a gradual changeover from the "all-purpose teacher" to the "single-purpose teacher." Let us try to show this changeover by stages:

APPROXIMATE PUPIL AGE RANGE IN YEARS	TEACHERS' ASSIGNMENTS IN TEAMS
4–5	Each teacher is a generalist, supported where possible by specialist colleagues. Each teacher is a scholar of at least one content area.
6–8	All teachers teach all subjects, but each has at least the beginnings of a specialty in one area.
9–11	Most teachers teach most subjects, but each has a well-developed specialty in one area.
12–14	All teachers have a well-developed specialty in one area plus enough strength in at least one other area to permit interdisciplinary collaboration.
15–18	Virtually all teaching is within a single area, though interdisciplinary collaboration is desirable.

In this listing, the word "specialization" is equated with subject-matter competence, as in the case of a teacher whose specialty is the teaching of science. Teachers may become specialists not only in a content area but in a methodology or technology, such as large-group instruction or small-group teaching, or in audio visual techniques. Also, when we talk about a science specialist or any other kind of specialist, we mean someone who has (1) a great fund of science knowledge per se, (2) a repertoire of methodological procedures specifically related to the teaching of science, and (3) general insight and information about the teaching process.

In that third category would fall most of what educators have lately been honoring as the "process goals in education": the competencies (tool skills, critical thinking, and techniques of inquiry), interests, and habits that are needed in the acquisition, evaluation, and utilization of knowledge. All teachers, generalists and specialists alike, should have a keen grasp of these goals and how they may be achieved at the successive stages of pupil growth. Only if they have such a grasp can the process goals serve as a common meeting ground for each team, across teams, and across schools.

TEAM TEACHING EXAMINED

The Extent of Its Development. It is difficult to estimate the current extent of team teaching in the schools, and it would be foolhardy to make any predictions. As in the case of nongraded schools, there are countless communities whose so-called team teaching arrangements prove on close examination to involve little more than token changes from the conventional. At the same time, there may be many unreported schools where the essential characteristics of team teaching are already operative. Therefore, statistics on the extent of adoption of cooperative teaching are extremely unreliable.

Some studies—for example, one conducted by the National Education Association's Project on Instruction in 1962—have predicted that about 30 percent of both elementary and secondary schools would have some form of team teaching by 1966. Without a doubt this is a highly exaggerated figure, especially if the "ideal conception" of team teaching serves as our criterion. Nevertheless, the overwhelming trend of the literature and information reaching educational institutions (such as the NEA) is that interest is increasing and that the self-contained classroom is rapidly being replaced by more flexible patterns of horizontal organization.

Lively interest in this trend has been shown by visitors from foreign countries. In a recent study, for example, members of the Alberta Teachers' Association predicted that team teaching would have more effect on Canadian education in the next ten years than would any other of seven new developments studied. Professor W. H. Lucow, then an Associate Professor at the University of Manitoba, predicted in a 1964 article that team teaching would take hold widely in Canada; that article has already been reprinted in English and Chinese in the Malaysian *Journal of Education*. Other parts of the English-speaking world have also shown great interest, and there is in fact one pilot project in the cross-cultural transplantation of team teaching already underway on the island of Barbados in the British West Indies. That project, by the way, is being directed by the former Director of the Norwalk Plan in Connecticut.

One regards such developments with mixed emotions, however, since the American experience with team teaching has thus far suffered from inadequate design, imperfect and incomplete development, insufficient research, and an almost total neglect of the optimum procedures for dissemination. On the other hand, the overwhelming majority of reports from pilot team-teaching projects have been so optimistic and encouraging that one is prompted to press forward.

The Tenor of the Reports. Much of what we said in chapter four about research in the nongraded school movement is relevant to team teaching. Most of the research studies have relied on questionnaires, and testimonial evidence from the three major groups involved (teachers, pupils, and parents) constitutes the bulk of data in hand. Most of the communities have also looked to the results of standardized achievement tests, of the sort that are customarily used anyway, in their efforts to determine whether the new arrangements have caused achievement levels to rise or drop. Only a few have applied other research designs. In general, we must conclude that far more suitable research procedures are needed. The following summary of findings, therefore, represents only a crude start in achieving a full understanding of the movement and its validity.

1. Teacher morale and attitudes Very little information has been assembled to show the effect of team teaching, with its more visible career line and its reward system, on the recruitment and retention of outstanding teachers. Some schools have reported a rise in the quality of both experienced and inexperienced candidates for teaching positions in team-organized schools, and colleges using team organization for the training of apprentices and interns have reported a similar upturn in both quality and enthusiasm; but at most these are promising straws in the wind. Projects making use of teacher aides and other nonprofessional assistants have reported a strong positive response from teachers and an increase in the professional competencies of teachers thus relieved of more routine and trivial functions. Projects employing a hierarchical structure have reported that it has been difficult to recruit, identify, and provide training for the persons needed in leadership and specialist roles. Some reports have attributed this difficulty to the strong equalitarian tradition among teachers, and others have linked it to the scarcity of persons whose university training has given them sufficient depth in a particular teaching field or in the skills of leadership.

Not surprisingly—because most were volunteers—the majority of teachers who have worked in teams express favorable attitudes and elect to remain in the teams. Even these volunteers, however, apparently undergo a rather severe and stressful period in adjusting to the demands team teaching makes on them. One argument in favor of team structure is that it is potentially more efficient and flexible—for example, with respect to the use of teacher time. In fact, though, the teams usually report an increase in both the amount of time spent during the working week and the complexity of tasks performed. Apparently this hardship has tended to "weed out" the type of teacher who is prepared to give only minimum energy to the job, but on the whole the reports suggest a strengthening of professional interest and a cheerful acceptance of the work load that arises.

A four-year report on the project in Pittsburgh indicated that the schools with team teaching experienced a reduced dependency on substitute teachers, a corresponding increase in the number of professionally qualified teachers, and a noticeable commitment to teaching as a lifetime career.

Nearly all teachers at the elementary level admit to initial reservations about sharing pupils with other teachers ("my class" becomes "our team"), but quite significantly these reservations appear to melt after the first four or five months. The efficiency of teams apparently varies with respect to the sharing of information and feelings about pupils, but, especially in projects where this function is emphasized, the teachers become convinced that they acquire far more data about their pupils than they do under the self-contained arrangement.

Teachers entering a team also tend to worry about maintaining discipline. Most projects have reported that discipline problems are minimized under the team approach. Lambert and his colleagues, in a careful study made in Wisconsin, found that the organizational framework of team teaching had less influence on discipline than did the school's overall attitude toward discipline and also (as might be expected) that interns suffered significantly more disciplinary infractions than did experienced teachers on the team.[18]

Teachers at all levels face a number of personal and strategic problems as they strive to work alongside one another, and the resolution of personality conflicts and related problems is admittedly not easy for the typical team. Many teachers suffer "stage fright" when they first perform in the presence of others, and nearly all team members tend to shy away from incisive critical discussions of one another's work. Apparently, however, the pleasures of work-

---

18. Philip Lambert, W. L. Goodwin, and W. Wiersma, "A Study of the Elementary-School Teaching Team," *The Elementary School Journal*, 66 (October 1965), pp. 28–34.

ing together and sharing information and techniques eventually override some of the interpersonal and other problems.

Lambert's report examines the arguments for and against hierarchical structure and states that in Wisconsin this structure was well received and successful. This confirms the author's experience in Lexington and elsewhere and leads to the observation that with further experience and development this aspect of the team idea can and will gain in general acceptance.

Ironically, people who take part in hierarchical teams tend to become strong supporters of the idea; the chief opposition comes from persons who have never experienced team teaching. Thus in some communities where hierarchical arrangements are working very well, pressures from the rest of the staff may lead to the abandonment or the modification of the arrangement.

Grace Gates, in reporting a team project based on the use of an experienced teacher in a limited supervisory role, concludes that team teaching is capable of promoting the mental health of classroom teachers and therefore "may assist also in the fostering of a generation of more secure and stable children who can cope more successfully with their school work." [19]

Not much evidence has as yet been reported on the changing role of the principal in the wake of the team-teaching movement. What little evidence there is strongly suggests that the principalship becomes a more challenging and complex role in schools where teams of teachers are at work. The author's personal observation, based on direct involvement in a hundred or more pilot programs, is that the greatest single factor in the success or failure of a team-organized school is the quality of the principal's leadership. Although the superintendent's support is also a vital factor, a mediocre or unenthusiastic principal can vitiate the support of an enthusiastic and effective superintendent. Similarly, principals have been known to perform miracles despite the lack of skill or support by the superintendent.

2. Pupil achievement and adjustment Almost without exception, pupil achievement as shown on standardized tests has been found to be about the same in cooperative teaching programs as in self-contained classrooms serving as control groups. To some this may seem a disappointing finding, but several factors must be

19. *Role of Supervisor and Curriculum Director in a Climate of Change,* The ASCD 1965 Yearbook, Washington, D.C.: Association for Supervision and Curriculum Development, 1965, p. 100.

kept in mind when such results are examined. To begin with, the available tests deal chiefly with the contents and skills that are least likely to undergo important changes in the early stages of team experimentation. The content areas in which livelier offerings and different pedagogical arrangements are more likely to be developed (such as social studies, science, and the arts) are rarely measured by the standardized tests in use, nor are pupil enthusiasm, pupil-to-pupil working relationships, pupil capacity for self-direction, efficient utilization of time, skill in locating and analyzing information, and other factors with long-range implications for pupil growth and achievement.

Probably the most dramatic contribution of research on team teaching has been to destroy some of the myths that surrounded the self-contained classroom as late as the 1950's, especially insofar as the personal and social well-being of pupils is concerned. Originally even its most enthusiastic promoters were not sure whether or not team teaching might have some undesirable effects on the personal security and the overall emotional and social well-being of the children, particularly the younger ones. Great caution was exercised in this respect, out of deference to the strong conviction within the profession that young children are in need of just one "mother hen" and a small, stable group of fellow students. In the Lexington project, the greater part of the research budget went into an examination of the personal and social adjustment of the pupils; the full-scale development of flexible grouping and other team arrangements was deliberately soft-pedaled with the early-primary teams.

It was therefore all the more surprising to the investigators when the evidence began to accumulate and the mother-hen mythology was exposed to glaring view. The Lexington and Norwalk projects in particular provided evidence that pupil adjustment was at least as satisfactory under the multiple-teacher, large-team arrangement as in the highly touted self-contained classroom. Many other studies also contributed to a general realization that organization per se is really not a causal factor in pupil adjustment at all, but that many elements must be taken into account as we examine why children are or are not happy in school. In general, more of these elements tend to be present in the more flexible and elaborate setting of team teaching, and therefore it now seems that the argument about self-contained classes versus teams can and will be replaced by the more sophisticated examination of group composition, teacher personality, pedagogical treatments, environmental conditions, and other variables and their differential impacts on pupils.

Meanwhile, it seems well established that team organization is capable of offering a congenial, hygienic, and stimulating atmosphere within which pupils can enjoy appropriate and meaningful affiliations with other pupils and with a number of adults, and within which pupils are likely to feel at least as comfortable and as happy as do pupils in more limited settings.

3. Parents' reactions Almost without exception, the pilot projects have reported strong support from parents, who in turn are a principal source of data about pupil interest and enthusiasm. Parents have proved to be far less addicted than teachers to some of the prevailing mythologies about self-contained classrooms; and although they are not necessarily willing to have their children "serve as guinea pigs," they have generally given wholehearted support to new programs in recognition of the prima facie evidence and arguments put forward by educators. Recently, as national magazines and newspapers have paid increasingly favorable attention to team teaching as one of the "good things" happening in education, the tendency has in fact been for PTA's and other parent groups to put pressure on conservative school administrators to undertake school reorganization.

The Pittsburgh project, which was conducted primarily in neighborhoods suffering from depressing cultural and socioeconomic conditions, reported not only favorable parental attitudes but important gains in the school-community partnership. Educationally supportive agencies and groups within the community made greater contributions to the schools and to the total development of children than previously, there was better communication between the parents and the schools, and there seemed to be higher morale in the school communities. In Pittsburgh and elsewhere, of course, huge problems remain unresolved, but gains of this sort are extremely encouraging.

Problems and Questions. We have already mentioned a number of matters that require further research. We are constantly reminded that team teaching at this stage can only be regarded as primitive and that theories and procedures must be further developed before the long-range usefulness and applicability of team teaching can be adequately evaluated. Heathers has rightly indicated that (1) almost all accomplishments to date belong to the design stage (that is, the planning and engineering of suitable team models); (2) none of the theoretical models currently being tested has yet been fully implemented (that is, there are still discrepancies between what is and what is intended); (3) the development and evaluation of team teaching are being impeded by a general failure to apply appropriate research strategies to the stages of design and implementation; and (4) the tendency of proponents (or for that matter, opponents) to argue the merits (and demerits) of team teaching, especially in advocating widespread dissemination and adoption, is therefore premature and unfortunate. Many years of exploratory development will be required, and more suitable techniques of research and evaluation must be utilized.

We still know very little about the group dynamics of team membership, about the relative costs of team teaching and alternative forms of horizontal organization, about the selection and training of personnel for teams (especially the leaders), about the differential values of team teaching for various categories of children, and especially about the various stages of development through which a school staff ought to proceed if an excellent team organization is eventually to emerge.

One of the most fertile areas for future study is the role of itinerant specialists (that is, teachers of art, music, physical education, homemaking, and other special services) in a team-organized school. These persons usually struggle under unreasonable work loads and unsatisfactory working arrangements. The public at large, and quite often the school administration, seldom appreciates the intellectual and other values of the "less-than-basic" subjects taught by these specialists. Generally, when the term "frills" is used, it is to these school experiences that the unenlightened are referring.

We cannot review the overwhelming evidence in support of these special subjects and their truly basic intellectual value, but we shall assume that such value exists. The problem, then, is: How can we maximize the services and contributions of the all-too-few teachers who teach these subjects?

Team organization is potentially a boon to the itinerant specialist, since it opens up more effective channels of communication to teachers and pupils alike. The team can schedule its pupils for special-subject instruction in a great many different ways, and all teachers can call on the specialist to deal at any time with large and small groups of pupils as need dictates. Furthermore, mutual involvement in the total school life of the pupils gives teachers a common meeting ground and opportunities to discuss pupils and programs that can only rarely be found in conventional schools.

Unfortunately, special teachers have over the years developed repertoires and curriculums that are geared almost completely to classes of conventional size. Even more than regular self-contained teachers, who frequently subgroup their classes and who sometimes combine classes or interchange pupils with each other, the specialists have fallen into the habit of dealing with twenty-eight to thirty pupils at a time. As a result, when they first encounter a team situation they tend to protect the familiar arrangement without pausing to realize that the team offers, in effect, a new opportunity for them. It is hoped that as time passes they will become more and more aware of the potential usefulness of large-group lessons, total-team lessons, and other arrangements that increase their direct contacts with pupils; at the same time they will learn how to enlist the help of the one or two members of each team whose talents and interests make them potential partners or assistants in the special curriculum area. This is one of the true frontiers of team teaching and one especially deserving of exploration.

Even more fundamental questions arise with respect to the total school program and the pressing need for major overhaul and reform. Once teachers start working together in the intense setting of the team, the full extent of the changes that are needed becomes overwhelmingly evident to them. The typical reaction of the conscientious team, once awakened to such need, is to roll up its sleeves and start tackling all the problems all at once. Eventually, of course, extreme fatigue and frustration are likely to engulf the team members unless steps are taken to limit and control the changes that will be attempted in any one month or year.

To pursue many of these changes independently and without recourse to the efforts of other professional groups is to invite trouble if not disaster. Teams must become more aware of and involved in the many curriculum studies being undertaken at the regional, state, and national levels. Shaplin describes as an "ominous sign" the fact that the team-teaching movement has thus far been relatively detached from such studies:

> Team teaching organization is only rarely being used as a vehicle for the introduction of national curriculum reform programs. . . . Characteristically, curriculum reform is proceeding on a local basis, with

enormous waste of energy. I doubt that the present pace, requiring
Herculean efforts by teachers, can be sustained on a long-term basis.
We need to build the connections between team organization and
curriculum reforms for their mutual benefit.[20]

Two other major questions arise: What effects does team teaching have on the roles of supervisors and principals? How is the
team-teaching movement related to the national enterprise of
teacher education? Obviously the answers to these questions, plus
the profession's response to Shaplin's challenge, will have consequences not only for the team-teaching movement but for the
future of the educational profession itself.

SUMMARY AND CONCLUSION

1. Though the current team-teaching movement may prove to
be only a major episode in the long struggle toward some ultimate
form of horizontal organization, it has all the earmarks of a historically significant event. It is in many ways a current phenomenon,
but it came about as the result of many events in which many educators participated over the greater part of a century.

2. Team teaching may exist in a variety of patterns, some with
loose or informal cooperation and collaboration, and some with
formal structure.

3. Teams of teachers engage jointly in planning, in teaching
activities whereby the plan is implemented, and in evaluation
of activities whereby both the plan and the skill with which it
was carried out are appraised.

4. The aspect of team teaching that is most unfamiliar to the
experience of American teachers and probably the most emotionally
loaded is its emphasis on full-scale, relentless evaluation. In the
conventional school, few teachers engage in intimate and continuous evaluative exchange with their professional colleagues. The
opportunity to exchange information and criticism and, hence, for
constant reexamination of the teaching role is almost certainly the
most powerful feature of the plan and a chief justification for its
energetic development.

5. Team organization theoretically allows for unusual variety
in the assigning, scheduling, grouping, and locating of pupils.

---

20. Judson T. Shaplin, "Cooperative Teaching: Definitions and Organizational
Analysis," *The National Elementary Principal,* 44 (January 1965), p. 20.

It permits many patterns and sizes of instructional groups to be organized. It allows for teacher specialization and at the same time compels (or at least attempts to compel) an integration of the total program for each child. It makes possible the relatively economical use of (and efficient supervision over) supplies and resources, physical spaces, and nonprofessional adult assistants.

6. Team organization has built-in supervisory potentialities—if by supervision we mean influencing the professional performance of a teacher through discussion, observation, and related procedures. Team teaching permits supervision through group work and cooperative efforts. It therefore offers opportunities for leadership to those career teachers who have talents in the supervisory (or exemplary and inspirational) area and at the same time provides a nourishing and stimulating atmosphere in which beginners and other teachers can work.

7. Team teaching is not in itself a methodology or a system for instructing. It is, rather, a stimulant to the analysis of instruction and to the development of needed technologies. In particular, it should lead to the invention or development of useful strategies vis-à-vis large group teaching, small-group teaching, and so-called independent learning.

8. Team teaching, similarly, is not a curriculum system. Rather, it tends to stimulate the reexamination of existing curriculums and the creation of new curriculum approaches. Such developments are independent of team organization as such, but the involvement of team members in the national curriculum effort is a high-priority need.

9. Teachers are by training or disposition unaccustomed to the patterns of small-group interaction characteristic of team teaching. The literature (mostly from fields outside education) dealing with social structure, social organization, communication systems, reward systems, leadership, morale, and the like has not yet been translated into operational guidelines for instructional teams.

10. Team teaching is linked both spiritually and functionally to the philosophy and the operational mechanism of nongradedness described in chapter four. Experience has shown that wherever teams of teachers have worked together in accordance with the ideas expressed in that chapter they have found it both necessary and possible to behave less like "sinners" and more like "saints" (see p. 53). That team structure has the effect of promoting

nongrading as a professional way of life may well be its ultimate value.

Suggestions for Class Discussion and Further Investigation

1. One of the arguments offered for team teaching is that the opportunity to serve as a team leader will attract higher-caliber college students into the profession and will retain them longer. Some of the attraction derives from the prestige and responsibility involved, some from the possibility of earning a higher salary. Are these factors of potential importance to you in your own career? Is it crass and materialistic to evaluate teaching from a salary standpoint? Does the leadership role have any attraction for you at this stage of your planning?

2. Filmstrips and sound movies are now available from various sources, and many of them depict team-teaching situations in action. Encourage your instructor to arrange for showings followed by class discussion. Of special interest is *This Is a Laboratory School,* produced by Professor Goodlad and his associates at UCLA. The NEA Center for the Study of Instruction can also suggest several items.

3. Shaplin has stated that for culturally disadvantaged children the team arrangement is virtually mandatory. Do you agree with this viewpoint? Would it be *less* necessary in a well-to-do community?

4. Has a clear distinction emerged in your own mind between conventional departmentalized organizations and the intra-disciplinary team as described in this chapter? In what ways do these forms differ—from the pupil's standpoint and from the teacher's?

5. Shaplin's comment that Hosic's Coooperative Group Plan "came before its time" leads to a question worth pursuing: Why was the idea well received in the early 1960's, whereas it had been rejected thirty years earlier?

6. George D. Stoddard, in *The Dual Progress Plan* (New York: Harper, 1961), has written an extremely sophisticated and convincing critical commentary on the self-contained class-room (see his Chapter 4, pp. 48–70). Read that commentary and compare it with the arguments offered for and against the self-contained arrangement in the present book.

Suggestions for Further Reading

Several textbooks dealing exclusively with the topic of cooperative teaching appeared in 1964. Of these, the practicing teacher will probably be most interested in Medill Bair and Richard G. Woodward, *Team Teaching in Action*, Boston: Houghton Mifflin, 1964. It draws on the authors' experiences in the Lexington teaching-team project, and it has an operational emphasis.

The Shaplin and Olds volume, *Team Teaching*, New York: Harper and Row, 1964, is the most definitive and scholarly treatment thus far available. The two editors have contributed four chapters summarizing the theory and the history of team organization, along with a taxonomy for team teaching. Joseph C. Grannis discusses team teaching in relation to the curriculum; Cyril G. Sargent examines school architecture; Dan C. Lortie discusses sociological implications; Glen Heathers analyzes team-teaching research and relates team teaching to the education reform movement; and Robert H. Anderson discusses various dimensions of organization, administration, and public relations.

Another useful book, growing out of Trump's work at the secondary level, is David W. Beggs III, ed., *Team Teaching: Bold New Venture*, Indianapolis: Unified College Press, 1964. It includes chapters by eleven other authors.

The bulk of the literature on team teaching consists of articles in professional magazines and various printed and mimeographed bulletins or reprints issued by colleges, school systems, and other agencies concerned with educational reform. In the latter group are the publications of the Wisconsin Improvement Program (1120 West Johnson Street, Madison, Wisconsin); the Oregon Program (Division of Education Development, Oregon State Department of Education, Salem, Oregon); the Staff Utilization Project of the Educational Research Council of Greater Cleveland (Rockefeller Building, Cleveland, Ohio); Harvard University's Center for Research and Development on Educational Differences (formerly SUPRAD; Larsen Hall, Appian Way, Cambridge, Massachusetts); the Instructional Programs Branch of the Division of Elementary and Secondary Education, U.S. Office of Education (Washington, D.C.); the Ford Foundation (477 Madison Avenue, New York, New York);

the Claremont Graduate School (Claremont, California); and various units within the National Education Association (1201 Sixteenth Street, N.W., Washington, D.C.; see especially the publications of the NEA Project on Instruction).

School systems whose team-teaching projects have been reported with unusual care and whose reports are available at moderate cost include the Reed Union School District (1155 Tiburon Boulevard, Belvedere-Tiburon, California); Norwalk Public Schools, Norwalk, Connecticut; New York City (Division of Elementary Schools, Board of Education of the City of New York, 110 Livingston St., Brooklyn, New York); and Pittsburgh (Division of Curriculum Development and Research, Board of Education, Pittsburgh, Pennsylvania).

Several bibliographies are now available in addition to those included in the texts and publications noted above. The Horace Mann-Lincoln Institute of School Experimentation (New York: Teachers College, Columbia University) published "Team Teaching: Working Bibliography" in August 1964, and released in July 1965 "Selected Bibliography Relating to New Patterns of Staff Utilization." Dr. Harold S. Davis of the Educational Research Council of Greater Cleveland published "Team Teaching Bibliography" in 1964. Robert H. Anderson's chapter in *Review of Educational Research* (October 1964), pp. 455–69, may also be helpful.

Of special interest is the entire January 1965 issue of *The National Elementary Principal,* which deals with cooperative teaching. This is an excellent, up-to-date "little textbook" in the field.

Finally, there is a growing literature on processes of change in education. Many of the textbooks and other writings in this field use team teaching as a major example. Special attention is called to Richard I. Miller, ed., *Perspectives on Educational Change,* New York: Appleton-Century-Crofts, scheduled for 1966 publication.

Chapter Six

The People
Who Work with Teachers

We have now examined some of the ways in which American schools are changing, particularly in organization. We have seen that teaching in a modern school involves a great deal more than standing before a group of twenty-five to thirty youngsters and lecturing or conducting a recitation. In our discussions of class and group composition, of the individualization of instruction, and of nongrading and team-teaching arrangements it has become evident that the life of a teacher is both more complicated and more interesting than many people realize. In this chapter we shall review some of the efforts that are being made to maximize teacher growth and efficiency and to provide supporting services and resources. In so doing, we shall try to shed light on emerging career roles (other than teaching) in the schools and on the ways in which existing roles are changing.

THE TEACHER'S COLLEAGUES

In the course of a typical school day the classroom teacher deals with many different fellow employees:

1. Colleagues who are engaged in essentially the same teaching activity as himself (for example, fellow team members or teachers within the same department) and with whom he has specific and immediate interests in common.

2. Colleagues whose teaching field complements or supplements his own and who, though they are essentially independent, work at times with the same pupils (for example, special teachers of art, music, physical education).

3. Colleagues who teach in another team or department, at another level, and with whom he has only general and school-wide interests in common.

4. Librarians, psychologists, and other specialists whose work may involve classroom teaching but whose function is primarily in a professional field other than teaching.

5. Principals, directors, supervisors, and others who are on a higher salary scale because, among other reasons, they are responsible for influencing and supervising the performance of teachers.

6. A broad category of nonteaching personnel (that is, persons who are not professionally certified as teachers, librarians, or supervisors), such as secretaries, custodians, and lunchroom workers.

A characteristic of the current scene in American education is that these roles are expanding and assuming more importance in the overall work of the regular classroom teacher. It may therefore be of interest to examine some of them, especially as they tend to enhance or increase the services, resources, and opportunities available to the teacher.

Partly because of the unique and growing importance of the librarian, and partly because it seems appropriate to link the librarian to our discussion of instructional materials centers and other space and equipment considerations, we shall postpone the librarian's story until chapters seven and eight.

ENTER THE NONPROFESSIONAL

Until recently the personnel structure of the typical school included only a few nonteaching roles: the school custodian, perhaps some cafeteria workers, a part-time nurse, and (in more fortunate schools) a school secretary assisting the principal. Left to the teachers as the chief manpower supply in the building were a great many functions not very closely related to instruction. Often these included a variety of janitorial and housekeeping chores plus tasks more properly performed by policemen, dieticians, bus drivers, office clerks, and trained medical workers. The job of "teacher" therefore came to have a very broad range of duties associated with it. Cynical or overimaginative administrators justified such duties by arguing that the teacher who dealt with the child directly or indirectly under a variety of circumstances became better acquainted with "the whole child" and was thus better able to understand his instructional needs. As a result, the teacher in America often spent a substantial portion of his working day at tasks other than those for which he was supposedly trained.

Although the incongruity and inconvenience inherent in this situation doubtless bothered the rank and file, there was surprisingly little evidence of rebellion or protest against the performance of nonprofessional tasks, even in the face of a postwar teacher shortage and a climate potentially favorable to professional reform. In fact, the silence and inaction on this problem within the profession and the very slow development of such obvious solutions as the expanded use of teacher aides remain both a discredit to educational leadership and a mystery to interested observers.

In this section we shall describe some of the studies that have been made of ways of separating teaching and nonteaching functions, as well as some of the recommendations that have been offered for establishing a full-fledged and respected cadre of nonprofessional and paraprofessional workers in the schools. Few of these recommendations, it must be admitted, have yet had much impact on school personnel practices, although some encouraging examples are already at hand.

There have been many attempts over the past 150 years to provide both preprofessional and subprofessional assistants for teachers. In the former category fall various arrangements for gradually exposing college students (teachers in training) to the teacher's role through an apprenticeship served under a teacher's supervision. Here would also be included those plans that call for the teacher to be assisted by older or brighter pupils in some formal way. The use of subprofessional assistants includes arrangements in which people who do not necessarily intend to follow a teaching career and who often have no college education serve in an assistant's role that calls for little or no special training or preparation.

A third category, sometimes called "paraprofessional," comprises persons performing tasks that might otherwise have to be performed by regularly certified teachers and that call for a certain amount of technical skill and training not ordinarily possessed by teachers. The term is used to cover a rather wide range of talents, some of which have less economic value than others. Persons with secretarial or clerical training (for whom the term "clerical aide" or "instructional secretary" may be used), commercial artists, specialists in audio-visual equipment or in instructional materials, so-called lay readers who read and evaluate student compositions, and some types of measurement and guidance workers fall into this general category. Persons without specialized training who

work at tasks explained and supervised by teachers (such tasks as
classroom housekeeping, the routine supervision of pupils in lunch-
rooms, and keeping attendance records), are ordinarily classified
as subprofessional rather than paraprofessional, and such terms
as "teacher aide" or "teacher assistant" are commonly used to identify them. We shall be concentrating on the clerically trained aide
and the general subprofessional teacher aide, sometimes imply-
ing that the same person may in fact be filling both roles simultaneously.

Prior to the 1950's a number of interesting projects involving
assistants for teachers were undertaken in Europe and the United
States. None of them had any notable influence on twentieth-
century American education, however, and not until the labor
shortage following the Second World War was much attention
paid to the teacher's multivariate role or to means of augmenting
the teacher force.

Most of the current interest in these topics owes its impetus
to two now-famous projects: (1) the Cooperative Study for the
Better Utilization of Teacher Competencies, conducted in the public schools of Bay City, Michigan, and other communities by
Central Michigan College, Mount Pleasant; and (2) the Yale-
Fairfield Study of Elementary Teaching, conducted in Fairfield,
Connecticut, under the guidance of Yale University. Both projects
were financed by the Fund for the Advancement of Education, and
the publications stemming from them have had a widespread and
significant influence on other projects. Among these are the
Catskill Area Project in Small School Design (with headquarters
at the State University College of Education in Oneonta, New
York); the Peabody-Public School Cooperative Program (out of
George Peabody College for Teachers in Nashville, Tennessee);
and a number of projects that incorporated subprofessional assistants or paraprofessional personnel in either educational television or team teaching.

Among the latter, the Norwalk Plan of Team Teaching, developed
in the public schools of Norwalk, Connecticut, is of special interest. In this plan the aide is completely integrated into the teaching team, and in a sense he takes the place of a certified teacher.
His role is carefully defined, however, so that he performs only a
specified range of general, clerical, and technical functions under
the supervision and direction of his teaching colleagues. Since
those colleagues are of unusual or above-average competence,

they are capable of carrying the somewhat heavier instructional load that falls on them.

In the Catskill Area Project and in various other programs, teacher aides and clerical aides are used to relieve individual teachers and groups of teachers of time-consuming tasks other than instruction. Often the reason for initiating this arrangement, as in the case of the Bay City study, is that class sizes and teacher work load have reached dangerous levels, and the siphoning off of routine duties is intended to relieve the burden. In the Norwalk Plan, aides are used in an effort to redefine the teacher function in more professionally attractive terms. In still other places, the assignment of aides to teaching teams reflects a decision to reinforce and relieve the teaching staff even at additional cost. This is true, for example, of the Lexington team-teaching project.

Why the Nonprofessional? With the foregoing section as background, let us now look more closely at the development of nonprofessional roles in American schools and why these roles have come into being. As we have seen, a variety of functions formerly assigned to regular teachers is now being considered for reassignment or delegation to people who have not been trained as teachers. This development may represent a significant change in the way schools will be staffed in the future. Is this consistent with what we believe to be good for the teaching profession?

Earlier, we defined teaching as an art-science calling for a high degree of competence along several different dimensions. And we have noted several times that no one teacher can be sufficiently skillful or knowledgeable to "be all things to all students." Each child in the school setting must have available to him a number of different people, each capable of responding in an appropriate way to one or another of his widely varying needs. Some of these needs are relatively trivial, and many are so specialized that not every adult on the school force can be expected to deal with them.

A basic concept, then, is that teaching and teaching-related functions are of different levels of importance and difficulty. Of all the things that teachers try to teach, and of all the services they and their colleagues are called on to perform, a significant number are relatively trivial (if educational significance is our criterion) or relatively simple (if difficulty of accomplishment is the yardstick). Others are neither very important nor very complicated; these are the tasks that a reasonably well-trained professional would regard as routine. Still others are rather important and require notable insight and skill to perform. Finally, some tasks are of the greatest importance and are extremely difficult to accomplish.

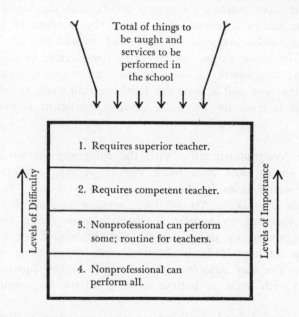

Note that category 1 in the figure is reserved for the superior teacher. If we were to use a medical analogy, this category would represent the surgeon at work in the operating room, the pediatrician treating an infant with a 103.5° fever in the middle of the night, the consulting physician interpreting a puzzling x-ray plate, the cardiologist studying an unaccountable deviation on an electrocardiogram. Category 1 in teaching terms is a social-studies teacher working to eliminate racial or religious prejudice or a science teacher devising a simpler way of explaining Einstein's theory to younger children. It is an English teacher deciding what to do with a creative young writer who cannot spell. It is a teacher talking to two angry boys pulled away from a playground fight two minutes ago. It is a mathematics teacher working with a mathematically gifted class or with a group of girls who openly dislike mathematics. Category 1, in short, represents teaching responsibilities too serious to be entrusted completely to teachers of average competence.

Category 2, to use our medical analogy again, would include the decisions and functions that are ordinarily restricted to licensed physicians. Not quite routine, but somewhat less demanding than those in our first category, these items would clearly require thorough medical training. In teaching, similarly, category 2 refers to items that could not (or should not) be attempted by untrained persons.

Category 3 includes functions that are neither so important nor so difficult as to demand more than a routine performance by a professional worker. In the medical analogy, these would include such matters as taking blood pressure, reading thermometers, checking height-weight records, testing reflexes, and reading blood counts—activities that are ultimately related to more important considerations but that scarcely require the energies or talents of a physician. More and more, the medical profession entrusts functions of this sort to specially trained nurses, technicians, and laboratory assistants working under a doctor's supervision. In schools, too, there are many tasks that do not require the immediate attention of a teacher and that can be performed by assistants working under a teacher's supervision.

Category 4 in our diagram represents activities of such low levels of difficulty and importance that there is no reason for the fully trained professional teacher to bother with them. In the medical analogy, these are the tasks always performed by hospital orderlies and attendants, student nurses, receptionists, and bookkeepers. In the school, they include such chores as the following:

1. *Housekeeping:* room care, lighting, and ventilation; care and preparation of chalkboards and bulletin boards; moving and arranging furniture, books, instructional supplies, and equipment; taking care of plants, exhibits, pets, and room decorations.

2. *Clerical work:* taking pupil attendance and maintaining routine pupil records, collecting and handling funds, taking care of routine messages and correspondence, typing and preparing materials for duplication and distribution, checking and correcting simple-response tests and workbooks, dealing with miscellaneous class interruptions, answering phone calls.

3. *Custodial-type supervision of pupils:* overseeing playground activities before and after school and at recess, maintaining order

at school bus loading and unloading areas, supervising hall and
stairway traffic, supervising the cafeteria.

4. *Routine personal help to pupils:* helping with clothing, administering minor first aid, making health checks, handling minor
discipline problems.

5. *Instruction-related activities:* writing on the chalkboard, supervising study activities, handling opening exercises, reading to
the class, dictating spelling tests or other teacher-selected materials
to the class, clarifying routine assignments, helping with pupil
projects, arranging for field trips, ordering films and supplies,
preparing materials for teachers, making library searches.

Although this is not a complete list, it suggests that teachers
have become saddled with a great number of tasks that waste their
time or that at least interfere with the performance of duties more
commensurate with their professional training and more appropriate to their salaries.

The Yale-Fairfield study revealed that elementary teachers spend
about 12 percent of their time on routine activities and another
7.6 percent on miscellaneous activities; a careful reading of the
project reports suggests that a substantial amount of additional
time is spent on the chores we noted in category 4 above. The Bay
City study indicated that elementary teachers spend between 11.7
percent and 18.8 percent of their time on clerical activities and
between 21 percent and 69 percent on activities that do not require professional competence. Further, when teacher aides were
introduced in Bay City, teachers on the average spent 23 percent
more time on activities closely related to instruction (for example,
144 percent more time on lesson planning, 80 percent more on
counseling) and 48 percent *less time* on activities *not* related to
instruction. Similar findings were reported by the Peabody Public
School Cooperative Program, in which the assistance given by instructional secretaries enabled teachers to expand the scope of
their teaching, make more adequate provision for individual differences, devote some 30 percent additional time to instructional
planning, and do a better job in testing and evaluation, public
relations, and other special functions.

Although the pilot projects have been reported in the literature
for at least a decade, there is no strong indication that the teacher-
aide idea is gaining in popularity. In a doctoral study made in
1960, for example, only about nineteen states reported the use

of paraprofessionals, and of these only Michigan, with thirty-seven such communities, had more than a handful of pilot projects. Oddly enough, enthusiasm for the use of nonprofessional assistants has not been noticeably great among school administrators or even among teachers. It is difficult to ascertain whether this lack of enthusiasm is a reflection of deep-rooted hostility to the idea or whether it is simply a bland lack of interest that may one day be converted into acceptance.

It would seem that lack of interest is now the case, although from about 1955 to 1960 there was a rather strong negative reaction to some aspects of the use of aides. The Bay City project, the first to receive extensive national publicity, met a cold reception in its early years. A typical reaction was the charge that using nonprofessionals would undermine the professional role. Other critics suspected that the use of aides was merely a means of justifying a higher pupil-teacher ratio, or that noncertified aides would dilute the quality of instruction and injure the well-being of pupils.

Another frequently voiced criticism was that children in the elementary schools might have difficulty getting along with and adjusting to more than one adult in the classroom. This argument was also being used against team-teaching programs. Similarly, concern was expressed about whether each teacher could really get to know "the whole child," an accomplishment that was presumed to be more difficult under conditions of shared responsibility. Still other critics raised legalistic questions, pointing out that the laws in some states apparently preclude nonprofessional employees from taking instructional responsibility, and warning that difficult questions about legal accountability arise when certain functions historically performed by teachers are relegated to others.

A few critics complained that personality clashes or other forms of friction might develop between teacher and aide. In retrospect, this seems to have been one of the least realistic complaints, since experience with pilot projects has been overwhelmingly to the contrary.

Over the years the other objections and apprehensions described above tended to disappear. After about 1960, in fact, the literature began to reflect rather strong support for the use of nonprofessional assistants and presented various counterarguments to the earlier criticisms. Most of this literature stemmed from specific projects, however, and neither the university scholars nor the school administrators' groups showed much interest in spreading the practice across the nation.

One explanation for this lack of enthusiasm is offered indirectly in a historical study by Raymond E. Callahan.[1] Tracing the impact of "scientific management" theories on educational administration in this century, Callahan notes that it became habitual for superintendents and school boards to emphasize economy-plus-efficiency (as opposed to true educational values) in school operations. Relating these developments to heavy teaching loads and large classes, among other undesirable factors, he suggests that educators have willingly subjected themselves to meaningless clerical work in an effort to please their finance-minded and efficiency-oriented employers. He notes that the training of administrators was dominated by such thinking in the 1920's and 1930's and observes that the survival of excessive clerical work and the willingness to perform it are probably explained by the fact that "administrators who were trained as bookkeepers in their graduate work . . . are still in key positions in our schools."[2]

Quite likely, too, many teachers and administrators derive satisfaction and comfort from performing clerical functions; these are usually discharged with relative ease, and, when they are carried out with accuracy and efficiency, they often bring disproportionate rewards. By contrast, to solve a real educational problem is usually far more difficult, and the accomplishment may bring no recognition or appreciation. Hence it is understandable that some teachers are reluctant to give up their routine, clerical functions and expose themselves completely to the hazardous functions of instruction. To define the satisfaction derived from teaching in such a trivial way is demeaning, but that fact has apparently been no deterrent.

Nor is it by any means clear where the line should be drawn between the functions that can and should be performed by aides and paraprofessionals and those that must be performed by fully trained professional teachers. Each published discussion of this topic sets somewhat different limits. There is little debate about assigning clerical and housekeeping functions to aides, but there is disagreement about assigning duties to them that call for face-to-face rela-

1. Raymond E. Callahan, *Education and the Cult of Efficiency,* Chicago: Univ. of Chicago Press, 1962, p. 273.
2. *Ibid.,* p. 178.

tionships with children. Much more research must be done on the teacher's role, the teacher-pupil relationship, and various patterns of task reallocation before questions of this sort can be resolved.

Aides in the Schools. Despite the lethargy of the profession over the expanded use of nonprofessional assistants, recent experiences with pilot projects offer many reasons for optimism. It has already been demonstrated that the use of aides enables teachers to concentrate on instructional planning and evaluation and enhances their morale and efficiency. Especially encouraging have been the high quality and the good supply of persons available for nonprofessional and paraprofessional roles. Working in the school setting and with the typical school calendar is both attractive and convenient for women in the local community, and many college graduates (sometimes even the holders of teaching certificates) seem pleased to serve as aides or assistants even though the salaries do not compare favorably with salaries in teaching. Most projects report that the employers are satisfied with the aides, and the low turnover rate suggests that employee morale is high.

Some of the people who accept nonprofessional roles have long-range professional goals; for them, experience as an aide serves as preprofessional training. Most applicants, however, appear to have no intention of going on to a professional career. There is no reason to believe that one or the other attitude is to be preferred, since both tend to assure the school of competent, loyal service.

For positions that require training in such skills as typing and bookkeeping, the school can turn to established business schools for recruits. It is more difficult, however, to fill positions that require competency in the use of instructional materials and equipment. Some local school systems, often with the help of commercial suppliers, have therefore set up their own training programs; this procedure is likely to become fairly standard unless colleges and training schools find it profitable to establish satisfactory programs.

One of the most interesting pilot projects in the use of paraprofessionals was conducted by Harvard University and the Newton, Massachusetts, Public Schools. Designed to help secondary-school English teachers extend their usefulness, this project used six lay readers (known as contract-correctors—that is, persons under contract to read and correct pupil compositions) as part-time assistants to the teachers. These lay readers were chosen because they had had college training and other experience in journalism or editorial work or because they were former English teachers. They received intensive preservice and in-service training, and they were carefully oriented to the standards and methodologies of the teachers they served. Working on an hourly rate in their own homes, they assisted in the grading of pupil compositions, met subsequently at the school with the teachers, and held individual conferences with pupils about their writing difficulties.[3]

Similar arrangements could be worked out in other secondary-school subjects. Some of the national testing services employ trained personnel to score essay examinations, and both written examinations and term papers could be competently evaluated in the local community.

Secondary-school teachers are often called upon to perform various extracurricular chores for which they have neither the time nor the background. One recent study of the workload of high-school teachers showed that teachers devote from one-fifth to one-third of their time to such duties. The school's efforts to provide a well-rounded activities program and appropriate recreational opportunities for its pupils are commendable enough, but there is no particular reason why the regular teaching staff should sponsor or conduct these programs. The chief reason seems to be that the teachers are already on hand! A greater effort should be made to recruit well-qualified persons from the community on a part-time basis to perform some of these special tasks.

Experience has shown that teaching teams are greatly strengthened when they include clerical aides, teacher aides, and other supportive personnel. Experience further suggests that a team of, say, five teachers can make more efficient use of one full-time aide than can five self-contained independent teachers sharing an aide. There is even evidence to suggest that schools could actually get along with fewer certified teachers if they used nonprofessionals to perform many of the tasks on which teachers now waste their time and talents.[4] However, in view of the tremendous backlog of unfinished business in most schools, and in view of the time and talents required for significant curriculum reform, it seems far more impor-

---

3. For a description of a similar program in the Cleveland Heights–University Heights (Ohio) City School District, see Leonard Freyman, "A-plus for Our Lay Readers," *NEA Journal*, 53 (November 1964), pp. 19–20.
4. Ellis A. Hagstrom, in an unpublished doctoral dissertation at Harvard University ("A Methodological Study to Assess Differences in Staff Utilization in Two Elementary Schools," 1960), suggested that six adults, two of them nonprofessional, could probably do as well for six classes of pupils as six teachers now do.

tant to argue at this point for supplementary personnel rather than for a cutback of some sort.

The need for nonprofessional supporting service varies from school to school and level to level. The school bus and the school cafeteria, for example, pose supervisory and coordinating problems in some schools, whereas other schools have neither bus pupils to load nor lunching pupils to oversee. We have already pointed out other ways in which need and load may vary.

Granted these variations, however, it seems that some minimum standards ought to be promulgated as a basis for national adoption of the teacher-aide idea. Just as it is widely accepted that all principals need at least one secretary to assist with the central-office load, should it not be agreed that every full-time teacher needs at least an hour per day of an aide's time? At least on a trial basis, this proposal deserves to be implemented. With each teacher (on the average) receiving five hours' service per week, a team of six teachers would have at least one person six hours per day. In situations demanding an unusual amount of in-service staff activity or higher standards of service to pupils, this allowance should of course be increased. While admittedly this scheme would require a significant additional cost, it seems clear that important advantages would accrue.

THE PART-TIME PROFESSIONAL

Related to the use of subprofessional and paraprofessional workers in the schools is a trend toward the employment of fully certified teachers on part-time contracts. We have already mentioned this idea, but we have not yet discussed hiring part-time teachers for regular teaching responsibilities.

Formerly teachers had to teach either full time or not at all. Now, however, many schools seek talented and trained professionals who can be on hand for only part of each day or week. These people may be guest lecturers or other unpaid resource persons, or, particularly in high schools, they may be people who teach or assist on a regularly scheduled part-time basis. Or they may be trained personnel acting as assistants to teachers, like the contract-correctors mentioned above.

One of the great advantages of the teaching team is that it can accommodate itself to the needs of the part-time teacher. In every community there are several persons, usually women with family responsibilities, who are qualified to teach but who cannot teach full time. The advent of team teaching has created new opportunities for such persons.

In Lexington, Massachusetts, for example, two part-time teachers were employed to fill one full-time position. Mrs. A taught in the morning, and Mrs. B taught in the afternoon. Their schedules overlapped at noontime, so that they had an hour or so for planning and consultation.

PARENT VOLUNTEERS

Partly because of the need in many schools for extra workers and partly because of a belief that school-home relationships are strengthened when parents play a role in the daily life of a school, it has long been a custom in certain school systems to use unpaid parent volunteers. These parents perform clerical functions, serve as library workers, help with cafeteria supervision, or assist the school nurse with health check-ups. Sometimes they provide actual teaching services such as tutoring. Many educators have misgivings about relying on unpaid volunteers, either because it seems unfair to exploit local citizens or because it is awkward to supervise and administer programs that depend on nonemployees. Many schools, however, benefit from such services and it seems likely that the use of volunteers will continue.

One of the best-known volunteer programs was launched experimentally by the Public Education Association in New York City in 1956 to provide classroom help for teachers. The arrangement succeeded, and it was formally incorporated into the school system in 1962. In 1964, 45,000 man-hours were contributed by 640 volunteers, and a Ford Foundation grant promised to increase the New York program in size and scope and to promulgate the idea nationally. The volunteers serve as teacher aides, helping to provide enrichment programs especially for pupils with high ability and special needs.

There is also a trend toward using volunteer assistants in team settings. The Reed Union School District (Belvedere-Tiburon-Corte Madera, California) has a new elementary building (Granada School) staffed by "volunteer instructional aides" in addition to various professional staff members and salaried team aides. The volunteer aides provide services equivalent to one and a half full-time workers for each team of about a hundred pupils. They help with library duties, the school health program (these are the "gray ladies"), and the instructional program. They assist the salaried aides by performing miscellaneous housekeeping functions, by providing receptionist and guide services for visitors, and by handling various clerical duties.

The team structure at the Granada School includes a highly experienced team leader, a team teacher (at the senior level) with average experience, a team teacher (at the junior level) who is a beginner, a salaried team intern, and one or two student teachers. Volunteers, however, are regarded as regular components of the staff.

Another interesting example of the use of unpaid helpers is reported from Washington, D.C. Here in a counselor-aides program launched in 1963, more than one hundred well-educated housewives spend a day or two each week visiting elementary schools in low-income areas and holding long (forty-five minutes, on the average) talks with children who need encouragement, help, or just a chance to say what is on their minds. Each counselor aide is assigned to three or more children and is expected to work with the children's parents as well. So far the program is reported to be working very well indeed.

CHANGING ROLES OF LEADERSHIP

Some of the most important changes taking place in the educational reform movement have to do with the leaders of the school system. To be a superintendent of schools in a time when American society is itself in a state of upheaval is both a great opportunity and a staggering responsibility. Today's schools often serve as the battleground on which some of the nation's most agonizing problems are fought out—for example, cultural deprivation, inequities of opportunity, the church-state issue, local versus federal control, the meaning and the mission of democracy, and controversies between interest groups. The school superintendent and his administrative colleagues are often in the middle of the battle.

At a less strife-ridden level, the growing complexity of school operations and the upsurge of interest in various organizational and technical reforms have created new opportunities and problems for leaders at the local neighborhood-school level.

Trump and others take the position that it is not very difficult to reorganize a school—to arrange the curriculum content, for ex-

ample, into a nongraded continuous-progress sequence and to eliminate the idea of literal self-containment among teachers. Given
our present knowledge and equipment, flexible scheduling, even on
a daily or weekly basis, calls for little more than routine administrative skill, as do the grouping and regrouping of students into
classes of varying sizes working in different spaces within the school.
The big problem is not changing a school's habits so that pupils
can spend more of their time in independent study, so that technical
instructional devices can be used more widely, and so that the staff
can accommodate a variety of nonprofessional and paraprofessional
workers.

The big problem, rather, is for teachers, administrators, and
supervisors to learn and to accept the new roles that these changes
demand. Trump observes that "unless [teachers] learn these new
roles, their teaching and the pupils' learning will be little better
than what has occurred in conventional classrooms for decades."
He argues further that "teaching roles, what pupils do in the learning process, and evaluation will be changed only to the extent that
teachers are carefully, correctly, and constantly supervised." [5]

One of the most emotion-laden relationships between the teacher
and his colleagues is the principal-teacher relationship. Dominated
as it so often is by the "management-worker" viewpoint, this relationship sometimes seems unpleasant and unproductive in the eyes
of the teacher. Since the principal serves as the agent of the employing school system on such matters as continuing employment and
professional recognition of the teacher's work, both parties inevitably feel some discomfort when certain events involving evaluation
or rules enforcement occur and when decisions about tenure and
salary are made. Often this discomfort is exacerbated when principals employ the wrong tactics or when their supervisory and administrative skills are unequal to the problems they confront.

Volumes have been written on this subject, and teachers have
spent long hours discussing it. Here we can only describe a few of
the ways in which the principalship itself is changing under the influence of the reform movement and suggest that the principal-
teacher relationship may itself undergo a fundamental revision.

The main responsibility of the principal is to provide leadership
in curriculum development and instruction. It is through "super-

---

5. J. Lloyd Trump, "Somebody Better Be Watching—Here Is Who!" *Phi Delta
Kappan*, 47 (September 1965), p. 38.

vision" (though to some the very term is offensive) that a principal tries to understand the professional strengths and limitations of his staff and to stimulate its professional growth. While the administrative duties of principals are important also, first priority should be accorded to the development of staff and program. As teaching becomes a more complicated activity and as the curriculum-reform movement moves into high gear, the person responsible for leadership in these fields faces an increasingly difficult task.

Some Basic Premises. In this book we have paid special attention to two important aspects of the educational reform movement. One of these is nongradedness, which we defined primarily as a set of guidelines for dealing with children. The other is team teaching, which we described primarily as a superior way to achieve efficiency and flexibility in the use of staff resources. We have argued that more truly individualized programs for pupils and more productive use of teachers' talents can be achieved when these arrangements are used in combination.

Now we turn our attention to the problem of how to make more sensible and productive use of the talents of principals (and other supervisors) in order that teachers may achieve higher levels of performance in their work. Let us consider two basic premises.

If nongradedness offers appropriate guidelines for teachers in their dealings with pupils, it may be equally useful in offering guidelines for principals in their dealings with teachers. That is to say, it should be possible to adopt the essential features of nongrading (as summarized in chapter four) as a basis for establishing each school's professional atmosphere.

If cooperative staff organization is appropriate and necessary in ensuring flexibility and efficiency among teachers, it may be equally appropriate in ensuring flexibility and efficiency among supervisors. That is to say, the suggestions offered in chapter five may be useful in joining supervisory forces and resources.

The first premise is less than revolutionary, given the present national climate. Much of the literature on supervision and administration takes for granted that individual differences exist among teachers and that in-service programs must be tailored to their individual needs. The second premise, however, is both revolutionary in itself and evocative of deeper understandings of the full import of the first premise. In my own experience, the idea springs in part from several summer training programs involving the clinical supervision of teachers by groups of supervisors-in-training.[6] It also springs from the revelation in pilot team-teaching projects of the great potentiality of cooperative organization for bringing multiple reactions and talents to the discussion of actual teaching performance. Yet these impressions did not come into sharp focus until the appearance of an article in 1964 by two men associated with a team-administration project in Palo Alto, California.[7] In this project, five principals proposed to share a variety of administrative and supervisory duties in five schools of roughly equal size, with a total of eighty-five teachers and 2,250 pupils. Each principal accepted leadership responsibility in one or more curriculum areas. Together, they coordinated the in-service training program and made "team evaluations" of teachers. Before long, another article appeared [8] that examined the underlying theories of cooperative administration and offered some plausible models. Various communities began to experiment with the idea on a small scale.

It is of course far too early to report on results, but I for one am persuaded that collaboration among principals and supervisors can contribute to the development of more effective leadership. From the standpoint of the principal, who otherwise faces a wide range of complex problems alone, much is to be gained from working alongside talented colleagues. Expert knowledge is shared, special problems receive group attention, various approaches are examined, and teacher evaluations can be validated. The various duties of the principal, especially those related to instructional supervision, become the topic of a continuing seminar in much the same way that pedagogical problems are discussed by teams of teachers. The more skillful and experienced principals become mentors of their "junior" colleagues in a setting that allows for healthy give and take.

From the teacher's standpoint there is much to be gained from exposure to a group of supervisors. Teachers often complain that teacher ratings (and other evaluations) are inadequate if not unfair because one principal may have less skill, knowledge, or even

6. Morris L. Cogan, "Clinical Supervision by Groups," *The College Supervisor,* 43rd Yearbook, The Association for Student Teaching, Dubuque, Iowa: William C. Brown, 1964, pp. 114–31.
7. Nicholas Anastasiow and Abraham S. Fischler, "A Proposal for Teaming Principals," *The National Elementary Principal,* 44 (November 1964), pp. 59–64.
8. James Greig and Robert R. Lee, "Cooperative Administration," *The National Elementary Principal,* 44 (January 1965), pp. 71–76.

motivation than another. Moreover, if a particular principal and teacher fail to get along with each other, an unbiased evaluation is unlikely. When evaluation is carried on by several principals, however, problems of this sort are reduced. Cogan points out that group supervision tends to reduce teacher anxiety and notes that, since a group possesses more persuasive power than a single individual, group supervision has greater value for the teacher.

It would seem, therefore, that cooperative supervision and administration is one of the most promising practices currently under consideration. It increases the services available to classroom teachers, and it provides continuous in-service growth opportunities for principals and supervisors alike. Venturesome school systems may well want to consider this arrangement and put it to a fair test.

Emerging Staff Positions: Research and Development. In March 1960, when the educational reform movement was still in its infancy, Philip H. Coombs of the Ford Foundation jarred the educational world with a provoking and timely question:

> What would happen if every public school system and every institution of higher learning had an able top official in charge of research and development—a "vice-president-in-charge-of-heresy"? His job would be to welcome fresh ideas, to encourage the trying out of new approaches in his school system or college, to evaluate the results, and to pass these on, good and bad alike, to colleagues in other school systems and colleges.[9]

Coombs's question came at a time when "research and development" (R&D) was being entrusted to the left hand (if to any hand at all) by the overwhelming majority of school systems. To be sure, the Ford Foundation had contributed a great deal through generous R&D grants to universities and forward-looking school systems, but the typical teacher in the early 1960's was very little involved in anything remotely connected with basic research and development. Among the few exceptions were those participating in some of the national curriculum projects and those whose degree programs encouraged on-the-job investigations.

The National Science Foundation injected large sums of money into teacher training and program reform, and as other federal

---

9. Philip H. Coombs, "Education's Greatest Need: A Vice President in Charge of Heresy," *Phi Delta Kappan*, 41 (March 1960), p. 246.

programs grew in size and scope a number of state departments of education and national organizations began also to expand their R&D activities. It remained for the remarkable achievements of the 89th Congress, however, to stimulate active involvement in R&D on a national scale.

The glacial rate at which the education profession as a whole has engaged itself in research and development is in embarrassing contrast with other professions and with the American economy in general. It has long been commonplace, for example, for business and industry to allocate generous resources to R&D, not only in the pursuit of new ideas and technologies but also in refining and developing policy. Some large corporations devote huge sums to personnel training programs, many of which resemble in quality and quantity the offerings of prestigious colleges and universities. The employees of such companies have at their disposal a rich curriculum, much of which is quite unrelated to their immediate or prospective work tasks but is offered in an effort to broaden their overall liberal education. Training programs with a vocational orientation are even more prevalent. These frequently are offered in conjunction with an institution of higher learning, as when prospective executives attend graduate schools at company expense or when a company brings in university people as instructors and consultants. Such companies feel that well-educated employees are a major source of corporate strength and new ideas.

In the more dynamic industries where the generation of new knowledge and the invention of new technologies is literally vital to a company's survival R&D activities commonly absorb one-sixth or even one-fifth of the company's total budget. In addition, substantial sums are spent on the supplies, equipment, tools, and other resources with which the employees work. By comparison, education devotes only a trivial proportion of its budget to personnel development, basic and applied research, and the resources on which the enterprise so desperately depends.

The National Education Association, through the NEA Project on Instruction, issued the following recommendation in 1963:

> School systems should allocate an appropriate proportion of their annual operating budgets—not less than one percent—for the support of research, experimentation, and innovation. Adequate time should be provided for each staff member to participate in curriculum planning, research, evaluation, and other activities designed to improve the instructional program of the public schools.

Probably the most startling thing about this recommendation, to anyone who is unaware of prevailing school budget practices, is that a figure of only *1 percent* should have been mentioned. The sad fact is that in 1963 only about *one-tenth* of 1 percent was being spent on such activities: the NEA was therefore proposing a tenfold increase!

It seems reasonable to assume that *at least* 1 percent of each school's budget ought to be earmarked for R&D activities, with perhaps a figure nearer 5 percent as a long-range target. Furthermore, a substantial portion of those funds should be allocated especially to services, resources, and training experiences designed to improve the quality of each teacher's day-to-day classroom performance. Additional funds beyond the 5 percent for R&D should be available for augmenting the school staff at the nonprofessional level and, where leadership is now inadequate, at the supervisory level as well.

It can be seen that serious involvement in R&D has important implications for classroom teachers and also for other personnel in the schools. New roles are being created, such as administrative assistants skilled in preparing and negotiating requests for R&D funds and other kinds of financial support at the local level. Moreover, school systems are appointing directors of research and program development, with functions similar to those of the "assistant superintendent for instruction" but geared more to research and planning. Similar R&D roles are being developed in state education offices, in state and national professional organizations,[10] and in state and regional agencies (for example, The Learning Institute of North Carolina). A number of universities are also becoming heavily involved both in developing innovative programs and in studying the processes of change in school systems.

In 1965, University City, Missouri, created the position of "specialist in educational organization and programming." Dubbed "the consultant in innovation," this person's main job is to act as a catalyst in speeding up change and to take an active part in formulating and implementing new ideas. He is definitely not to be a public relations man, though his success obviously depends on his

---

10. The Massachusetts Teachers Association recently created the position of a "coordinator for instructional services" who is to plan a center for instruction along the lines of the NEA project recommendation. Massachusetts is the first state in the nation to implement a major recommendation of the national project.

being able to earn the confidence of teachers and administrators through continuous contact and discussion.

Other school systems will clearly adopt a variety of arrangements for encouraging and facilitating change in the years ahead. It is to be hoped that the entire structure of public school administration, as well as the related enterprises of personnel training and R&D at the university level, will become more effective as American educators acquire skill in planning and implementing educational innovations. Already the scholarship and literature in this field are growing.[11] Among the forthcoming contributions will be a definition of the roles that have been emerging and a redefinition of the familiar leadership roles (especially that of the principal) on which the major burden of educational progress will continue to fall.

Suggestions for Class Discussion and Further Investigation

1. The next time you visit a classroom, keep a record of the teacher's various activities, using the diagram on page 114 as a guideline. In the period covered by your visit, try to estimate the amount of the teacher's time and energy being consumed by the routine and simple tasks in categories 3 and 4. Determine whether these tasks could in fact have been delegated to a nonprofessional assistant without loss to the teacher's own role and purposes.

2. It is sometimes argued that teachers are reluctant to give up some of the duties in categories 3 and 4 because (a) these duties are easy to perform and (b) sometimes they provide the only real sense of accomplishment if teachers are less skilled in the professional realm. Do you agree with these arguments? Are there more legitimate reasons for teachers to occupy themselves with the routine functions?

3. Talk with some teachers about the use of teacher aides in the schools. Try to determine whether there is any effort among

11. A standard volume in this field since 1958 has been *The Dynamics of Planned Change* by Ronald Lippitt, Jeanne Watson, and Bruce Westley, New York: Harcourt, Brace, and World. Other useful books are: Warren G. Bennis, Kenneth D. Benne, and Robert Chin, *The Planning of Change*, New York: Holt, Rinehart and Winston, 1961; Richard O. Carlson, et al., *Change Processes in the Schools*, Eugene, Oregon: The Center for the Advanced Study of Educational Administration, Univ. of Oregon, 1965; Richard O. Carlson, *Adoption of Educational Innovations*, Eugene, Oregon: Univ. of Oregon, 1965; Matthew B. Miles, ed., *Innovation in Education*, New York: Bureau of Publications, Teachers College, Columbia Univ., 1964.

the local teacher group to request an increase in the provision of aides and assistants for teachers. If it seems that the teachers are not very aggressive or concerned about this matter, try to find out their reasons for accepting the status quo.

4. In this chapter it was suggested that teachers may prefer to be evaluated by several principals rather than just one. Does this seem to be a reasonable argument? In what ways would a teacher's life be improved or modified if he found himself dealing with *several* principals or supervisors?

5. What is likely to be the effect of emerging R&D roles upon the general attractiveness of careers in education to students now in college and high school? Are competent young persons more likely to enter teaching if they see it as a potential first step toward a variety of R&D roles?

Suggestions for Further Reading

The references cited in footnote 11 are of particular interest to persons exploring the change process and ways of introducing educational innovations.

The publications of the Yale-Fairfield Study of Elementary Teaching, though not of recent origin, remain among the best available materials on the work of the teacher and the use of teacher assistants. Both the *1954–55 Report* (published in February 1956) and the volume entitled *Teacher Assistants* (1958) have been issued in abridged editions. If your library does not have copies, write to the Fund for the Advancement of Education, 477 Madison Avenue, New York, New York.

Chapter Seven

The Changing American Schoolhouse

The educational reform movement in America, as elsewhere in the world, has come during a time of rapid population growth. Although not all the cities of the United States are growing in size, most of them are expanding and spilling over into suburbs, and nearly all are faced with problems of renovation and renewal. Even isolated rural areas are stirring as small industries spring up and as small, inefficient school districts consolidate. Few taxpayers are free of the responsibility to build new schools for the ever expanding school enrollments and to renovate or replace school structures that are no longer suitable.

The professional life of every classroom teacher is profoundly influenced by the space in which he works and by the overall physical environment of the school. Such special facilities as the library are becoming more and more important to the accomplishment of the teachers' goals for children. Moreover, new instructional materials have implications not only for the teacher's pedagogical behavior but for the architecture of the school itself. These and other matters we shall discuss in the last two chapters of this book.

Space does not permit us to review the various architectural, engineering, and manufacturing advances that have revolutionized the shape and structure of school buildings. Today one sees dome-shaped schools, schools without exterior windows, schools located in skyscraper buildings, schools whose libraries are larger than their gymnasiums, schools spread out campus-style on large plots of land, schools whose classrooms are virtually without walls, and schools as radically different from the little red schoolhouse as Shea Stadium is from old Ebbets Field. One even sees schools with air conditioning, floor carpeting, and private offices (or their equivalent) for teachers and pupils.

Despite these innovations, however, school architecture in Amer-

132

ica is still not the flourishing art it deserves to be. Most American schools are still sterile, unattractive, uncomfortable, and inflexible. The very fact that many new school buildings have won journalistic attention is evidence that interesting design, striking beauty, and functional suitability remain newsworthy (that is, rare) attributes whenever they are found in a school. Many people, in fact, are suspicious not only of the probable fiscal extravagance involved but of the educational legitimacy of school facilities that combine grace with versatility.

The greatest progress to date has not been in school design but in engineering and equipment. The organic functional features of schools have, understandably, changed more fundamentally and quickly than have the form and shape of the buildings themselves. This is not altogether the fault of the architects, since communities have given architects less freedom than they have given engineers and equipment designers. The full genius of the architectural profession has yet to be released in the design of school buildings.

THE PLANNING OF SCHOOLS

The stages through which school architecture has gone in the United States and abroad and the techniques that have evolved for determining school needs and carrying out school building projects are the subjects of a growing literature.[1] Although these matters are of greater interest to school administrators and officials than to teachers, it is important for teachers to understand and to take part in school planning. Much of what they do is affected by the equipment and facilities available to them.

As in the case of teaching itself, the success of school planning depends on how well the objectives of the enterprise have been examined and defined. Simply to copy someone else's plans for a lesson or for a building or thoughtlessly to carry forward habits and procedures to which one has become accustomed is neither sensible nor safe in a time of rapid change. Yet the great majority of school buildings under construction even in the 1960's have been projected in this manner. It is highly unusual for school districts to invest appropriate amounts of energy and talent in the formulation of modern, educationally sound specifications for schools.

---

1. An excellent overview is provided in *The Cost of a Schoolhouse*, New York: Educational Facilities Laboratories, 1960.

On the contrary, the typical school building project is based on specifications that say little or nothing about *educational* requirements and that provide the architect with little insight into the ways in which teachers in future years may wish to group their pupils, individualize instruction, utilize audio-visual and autoinstructional devices, and create what we defined earlier as a nongraded psychological and operational atmosphere. Usually, school officials simply state that they want fifteen (or so) classrooms, a gymnasium, offices, and so forth; they also set down various details concerning plumbing, floors and ceilings, ventilation, lighting, and site development. And, probably, they warn the architect about the need to economize by avoiding expensive frills and materials. As a result, school architecture only occasionally rises to the level of a high art form, and rarely is the new school a truly functional, flexible structure.

Although flexible grouping patterns, cooperative teaching, and related organization plans have not yet gained complete acceptance, it seems clear that such patterns will dominate school practice in the future. This means that the "egg-crate" school designs prevalent in the United States will soon be functionally obsolete and billions of American tax dollars will be wasted on new but inflexible structures unless teachers and others awaken their communities to what is happening.

Every school system can guard against physical obsolescence by avoiding strictly conventional designs and by demanding flexibility and convertibility in its new schools. In addition, it can provide for the installation of air conditioning to permit year-round comfort, the ultimate use of computerized instruction and recordkeeping, the extensive use of television and other electronic or mechanical devices for instruction, the setting up of instructional materials centers with provisions for individual projects and study, and the expansion or rearrangement of space as needs and conditions change. Some ways of providing for these features are discussed below.

Officials Who Influence School Planning. In 1953, sociologist Neal Gross of Harvard University conducted a study of school administrators in Massachusetts. He found that in their own opinion and in the view of their school board members, the superintendents were doing their best work in finance, personnel, and school plant management and their poorest work in directing instruction. This situation is reflected in the nature of training programs for school administrators, which at least until recently tended to emphasize business management, accounting, purchasing, the operation and maintenance of school buildings and equipment, public relations, and other mechanical aspects of the school enterprise. It is also reflected in the topics included in the textbooks, magazines, and other publications aimed at school administrators. The business-management dimension of the superintendent's work is, in short, more dominant than the analysis of educational policies and the charting of new educational directions.

Similarly, school boards consist primarily of businessmen and other community leaders whose competence and interests are more likely to lie in administrative management than in educational policy. Moreover, the pressures on school boards and their executive officers usually center on management matters: the cost of schools and rising tax rates; policy on school neighborhoood lines, bus transportation, pupil food services, and pupil safety; salary policies for teachers and other employees; the preparation and supervision of the school budget; and related legal and political problems. As a result, school boards tend to emphasize school-management matters in their dealings with superintendents, and the superintendents' efficiency in such matters is often rewarded more generously than is their effectiveness in educational leadership.

It is in this general context that we must examine what happens when school buildings are being planned. All too often the community's chronic concern with school costs leads the community to postpone essential programs and school facilities until an urgent situation arises. All too often, the burden of daily operations keeps top-level administrators from consulting with their staffs about the educational changes that they ought to be undertaking. All too often, as a result, the realization that new or renovated facilities must be built finds the staff unprepared to define its physical needs.

And so, in what amounts to quiet desperation, the staff reaches into its past records and experiences and says to the architect, "Give us some more of the classrooms we are used to."

Nor is it likely that the local community will receive much help from state and national agencies. In most states, school building codes are distressingly obsolete, and the engineers and other officers who enforce them are of the old guard both in their training and in their attitude toward technological progress. Many code provisions protect the vested interests of building trades and manufacturing industries, and efforts to change them meet with powerful opposition. Even within state departments of education and national organizations concerned with standards for school planning and procedures, the old guard occupies most of the powerful positions and the unions and manufacturing interests are effectively represented in the policies and practices that are set down.

It would be unfair to imply that these influences are always sinister, but it does seem true that in matters affecting the planning and construction of schools considerations other than pupil welfare play too large a part.

What do we mean by the old guard in state offices and national organizations? We mean people who have, for the most part, received their training and practical experience during a time when schools contained classrooms of uniform size, when instruction was seen as primarily a didactic enterprise, when school architecture was barren of imagination and leaders, when Frederick Taylor's concepts of "scientific management" dominated school administration, when the materials and technologies available to architects and engineers were primitive compared with those now available, and when the state's relationship to local school systems was primarily one of inspection and control rather than one of giving advice and assistance. Such men find it difficult to alter their ideas about what a building should be like, about what teachers can and cannot do, and about how laws and codes should respond to the achievements and needs of children.

Therefore local school boards are unlikely to receive encouragement when they seek state support for a new and different building. Nor are they likely to be encouraged to seek more flexibility and alternative architectural solutions when they come up with plans for a nice, new, obsolete, and inflexible school.

Another conservative force on the national scene is the influence exercised by consultants in school administration and building planning. Raymond E. Callahan has written a fascinating and disturbing account [2] of what happened to school administration between 1910 and 1929 when the scientific management ideologies and technologies of the business and industrial world were imposed on education, and when educational questions were subordinated to such business considerations as efficiency and cost accounting.

---

2. Raymond E. Callahan, *Education and the Cult of Efficiency*, Chicago: Univ. of Chicago Press, 1962.

In Callahan's view, the consequences of these events for American education—and, in fact, for American society—were tragic. This period produced great and powerful administrators who were not really educators, and these leaders in turn influenced the training and experience of many men who are still actively engaged in school administrations or in other key roles (e.g., officials in state departments and professors of education). Consequently, Callahan concludes, the business-managerial conception of school administration persists in the 1960's.

Many school consultants, of course, are admirably equipped to offer *educational* as well as business-managerial advice on the planning of school buildings and related tasks. Many of them, however, are the professional descendants of the men Callahan described. They come with briefcases full of useful information about rubber tile versus vinyl, the number of square feet needed for a boiler room, the best windows for a southern exposure, the equipment needed for a cafeteria, and the best location for the music room. Their knowledge and interest in the fundamental educational questions that underlie school-planning decisions in the 1960's are often far less than their technical knowledge.

One of the best-known consultants in the business worked recently in a community that was making ready for a new high school. The superintendent reported afterward, his eyes wide with disbelief, that throughout the entire proceedings this giant among consultants never even mentioned small-group instruction on his own initiative! This man's firm uses such phrases as team teaching and nongraded schools interchangeably and loosely in its documents, and its recommendations rarely go beyond perfunctory acknowledgment of the effect individualized instruction is likely to have on the library area and other spaces. Some other consultants equate team teaching with large-group instruction.

The Need for Better Planning. Clearly, then, it is necessary for classroom teachers, librarians, and other educational specialists to play a larger role in the planning of future schools. Administrators, school-board members, state officials, and building consultants tend to understate the need for flexibility, and they must have the benefit of the insights and suggestions that creative and up-to-date teachers can provide. Since not all teachers are either creative or up to date, however, the burden of this responsibility will probably fall on the more professionally minded and pedagogically oriented teachers in each school system, to whom of course many other leadership obligations accrue as well.

THE PROBLEM: ADAPTABILITY TO CHANGING NEEDS

Not so long ago it was relatively easy to specify the kinds and sizes of space a school needed. Loyalty to the self-contained classroom, confidence in the desirability of class sizes between twenty and thirty, and an attitude of cheerful compromise toward various supplementary space requirements (library, offices, multipurpose rooms, and so forth) combined to persuade school administrators that what they needed was an "egg crate" of equal-sized compartments plus modest auxiliary facilities. And this, of course, is what the architects gave them.

Now the situation is radically different. School practices are in a state of flux, and, although the general shape of tomorrow's schools is at least vaguely apparent, there are many unanswered questions. We do not know, for example, how the computer and other technological devices will influence instructional programs in another twenty or thirty years. Nor do we know as much as we must about pupil grouping, methods of presentation, evaluation of pupil performance, and other factors that may influence school design in the future.

Therefore, one of the chief requirements in the planning of new schools is that they be adaptable to conditions that cannot yet be foreseen. We are asking, in fact, that our new buildings be (1) suitable for team teaching and other procedures at their present stage of development, (2) easily adaptable to the probably more radical developments that seem to lie ahead, and (3) suitable for the conventional programs to which many teachers are still loyal, and to which we may some day elect to return if the educational reform movement should fail. Little wonder that architects have had such difficulty in understanding our problems and interpreting our needs.

Expansibility: Permanent and Temporary.   There are several ways of looking at adaptability or flexibility in school structures. For instance, capability of enlargement by temporary or permanent additions is desirable whenever school enrollments promise to increase or future improvements of the plant itself are contemplated. Architects usually have little difficulty in making provisions for future expansion when doing the original design, but sometimes an exciting building that was not planned for expansion presents a frightful problem when a community wants to enlarge it.

Inventive designs and new approaches to construction and transportation have in recent years boosted the use of temporary, relocatable school buildings in solving the problem of space shortage. In some cases, temporary structures are used as a stop-gap measure pending the construction of permanent quarters. In other cases, temporary buildings are used to meet a temporary need, as where the school population is expected to stabilize at a lower figure. Or they may be used to cope with population shifts from one neighborhood to another. They help to provide such supplementary spaces as mobile libraries, learning laboratories, extra office space, storage areas, lecture rooms, and kindergarten classrooms. Temporary facilities are usually less satisfactory than permanent quarters, and they are not always economical in the long run. But often they are entirely suitable and they add valuable and functional space to existing schools.

Educational Facilities Laboratories has prepared a useful and interesting analysis of developments in the field of relocatable school facilities, including case studies from twenty-one communities across the country.[3] This analysis points out that facilities may be portable (designed to be moved as a unit), mobile (mounted on a trailer, bus, or truck chassis), divisible (movable in segments), divisible-mobile (movable in halves, with each section mounted in the manner of a house trailer), or demountable (capable of being dismantled and relocated). The statement concludes with an imaginative proposal that deserves widespread consideration.

The key idea of the EFL proposal is a convertible classroom-commons core that forms a permanent part of the regular school and contains all the necessary connections for utilities and heat supply. The core is approximately the size of three classrooms and can be used as regular classroom space until "satellite" classrooms are added to the perimeter. At that time the core area can become a commons area for large-group instruction, library facilities, and other purposes. It is possible over the years to add five or six satellite spaces of varying size, and mobile facilities can be brought to the school as needed. If school enrollment declines, the satellites

3. *Relocatable School Facilities*, New York: Educational Facilities Laboratories, 1964.

can be relocated at another school with a similar core unit. The use of operable walls and acoustical carpeting provides a versatile and comfortable atmosphere. Through arrangements of this sort a school district can achieve an unusual degree of flexibility while maintaining high standards of quality.

Other Types of Flexibility. In addition to expansibility, a modern school building should possess other kinds of flexibility. First, it should be versatile—that is, it should lend itself to a variety of uses, both immediately and over the long run. Second, it should be capable of on-the-spot internal rearrangement (some architects use the metaphor "malleable" to describe this quality) with minimum effort. It might, for example, have folding partitions that permit spaces to be combined or separated. Third, it should be capable of economical modernization when educational requirements change. "Convertibility" is the term generally used for this kind of flexibility.

There are several ways to achieve these kinds of flexibility. One is to build a school with a variety of spaces, each suited to a different function. An example of such "planned variability" is the Estabrook Elementary School in Lexington, Massachusetts. One of the first buildings specifically designed for team teaching, Estabrook is equipped with an amphitheater-type room for large-group instruction, a wing with six permanent (but convertible) small rooms of about three hundred square feet each, a study center adjoining a large library, a separate work area for team teachers and for nonprofessional aides, and several clusters of conventional-sized classrooms. Thus, architectural provision is made for each of the specific functions and activities that are central to Lexington's concept of team teaching.

A second way of achieving flexibility is through the use of the so-called loft plan. Here the architects locate roof-supporting and other load-bearing partitions in such a way that the interior space of the building is left relatively free and open. It is then possible to subdivide the interior space by means of operable walls or movable partitions which, when retracted, provide one or more large unrestricted spaces. These spaces can then be used for large, medium-sized, and small groups with relatively little difficulty or loss of time. The great majority of new schools in which provision is being made for flexible grouping have chosen the loft plan.

Yet another way of achieving flexibility is to deny the need for any space partitions either permanent or temporary. Open plans have become increasingly popular in the past few years, and in a later section we shall look more closely at "schools without walls." Among the earliest examples of this venturesome arrangement were an elementary school in Carson City, Michigan; a high school in Andrews, Texas; two middle schools in Saginaw, Michigan; an elementary-school addition in Chagrin Falls, Ohio; Dilworth Elementary School in Cupertino, California; and a dome school (based on a plan originally developed in 1960 in Port Arthur, Texas) in Queens, New York.

MEETING EDUCATIONAL DEMANDS

Earlier, we defined teaching as a highly professional role based on both artistry and science. We emphasized the importance of professional colleagueship and stressed the need for teachers to work and plan together and to exchange professional ideas and criticism. If curriculum-building and professional study are to be major ingredients in each teacher's working life, it follows that a school must be designed and equipped in such a way that teachers will be able to work both alone and in groups. A desk in a corner of a classroom, surrounded by bustling students, is scarcely sufficient. There must be a separate area, preferably convenient to the materials, books, and equipment needed for planning, where each teacher can have his home base and where team conferences can be easily organized. Whether there should be several such locations, one for each team or group of teachers, or a larger centralized location for the entire school staff, depends on such factors as the size of the school, the way the building is laid out, and the way the staff is organized.

We have argued that nongraded organization and various related provisions are essential to truly individualized instruction. Nongradedness in itself has little direct bearing on school architecture, but the related considerations of pupil grouping and independent study have an obvious and significant bearing. Similarly, a large and well-equipped library-instructional materials center should be at the heart of the school building.

Cyril G. Sargent has pointed out that schools with team teaching must provide not only for groups of varying size but for the effortless flow of pupils from space to space with a minimum of commotion and confusion.[4] To achieve a suitably "fluid" school, the architect must understand how teachers and pupils are likely to organize their daily lives.

The designers of new schools should also pay more attention to curriculum areas that are generally short-changed in the school program: health and physical education, the creative and expressive arts, and the arts and skills that are related to living in the home. Only rarely do schools include spaces where special teachers and other workers (counselors, speech correctionists, remedial reading specialists) can perform their tasks. Good school planning should make such provisions.

Equipment, Furnishings, and Appurtenances. The American Association of School Administrators at its convention in Atlantic City, New Jersey, sponsors an exhibit of school supplies, equipment, and furnishings. Anyone who encounters this mammoth display for the first time finds it a truly overwhelming experience. One comes to appreciate not only the size and the economic importance of education-related industries, but also the resourcefulness and the competitive zeal with which the suppliers are responding to the changing needs of the school market. Here are arrayed textbooks and printed materials, audio-visual devices of many types, school furnishings, supplies for cleaning and maintenance, school buses, office equipment, engineering equipment, and countless other items.

From the furniture exhibits one learns that there are now many different styles of "working stations" for pupils: individual tables or table desks (of various shapes) with chairs, combination seat-chair units, chairs with tablet arms and storage attachments, tables for two or more pupils, and several different types of study carrels. Many of these units, and the general-purpose tables (again of various shapes) that supplement them, can be stacked on top of each other for convenience in storage and cleaning. Some of them are adjustable in height, although the industry has yet to develop first-rate mechanisms for changing the height of standing equipment.

Several different types of chalkboard and writing surfaces are to be found in a variety of colors. Display surfaces come in corkboard, tackboard, punched wall-board, and easel-type finishes. Some of

---

4. "The Organization of Space," *Team Teaching*, Judson T. Shaplin and Henry F. Olds, eds., New York: Harper and Row, 1964, p. 220.

these units are demountable and interchangeable, and it is not uncommon to find installations whose height can be changed as needed.

Probably few teachers pay much attention to the size and adjustment of classroom furniture, except perhaps at the opening of the school term when seat assignments are being made. The proper fitting of desks and chairs to pupils has become a rather severe problem in recent years, however, because of team teaching and other arrangements that cause children to move about the building frequently. The problem is further complicated by multiaged grouping plans and other procedures that call for children of different ages and sizes to inhabit a room throughout the day for a variety of purposes. Many children find themselves using furniture that is too big or too small, and possibly even dangerously so. Teachers and other workers are obliged to see that such hazards and inconveniences are eliminated.

The furniture requirements of every class or team of children should be checked at least once each semester. For every child at a given moment there is a chair height and a table or desk height that is most appropriate and comfortable. A good plan is to order chairs and desks in a variety of colors, each color representing a particular size. For example, all thirteen-inch chairs are blue, all fourteen-inch chairs are yellow, and so on. Existing furniture can be coded by means of decals, colored adhesive tape, or other markings. Each child can then choose a comfortable seat when he enters a room.

Some teachers find that the furniture that has been provided is too small for some children. American children are growing taller and larger, as indeed are children in many other countries,[5] and orders for new school furniture are often based on morphological data for the preceding smaller generation. Classrooms used by several groups of children may have to be furnished with a generous supply of furniture, some of which can be easily stored or stacked, in order to meet all requirements.

Another problem in schools where pupils move about freely is that of providing easy access to loose supplies and equipment. Pupils in self-contained classrooms usually have an assigned desk in which

---

5. In Japan, for example, the average height of primary-school children increased about two inches between 1950 and 1962, while that of junior-high children increased about three inches. Standards for school desks and chairs, based on height-weight charts dating to 1921, have had to be revised substantially.

they keep crayons, paper, rulers, pencils, personal books, and other items. With a team organization, teacher-provided supplies of this sort must be available in each classroom, and the children must have some convenient way of carrying their materials about. Several manufacturers provide trays, boxes, bags, and other containers for this purpose, although homemade containers may be just as satisfactory. Suitable storage space must be provided in each classroom for the various products and projects on which the pupils are working (such as unfinished art work or science experiments).

Many modern classrooms have movable or portable bookcases and cabinets, sometimes mounted on casters. Book trucks, magazine display racks, easels, display boards, and other movable items sometimes serve as temporary walls or space dividers when the teacher wants to provide privacy for small working groups. The same results are obtained by use of movable wall surfaces attached to a permanent wall. More elaborate means for dividing space are folding partitions, operable walls, and other fixed-track dividers.

Many schools designed for cooperative teaching and unconventional pupil-grouping patterns use operable or folding walls to provide acoustically protected spaces for small working groups. In combination, these spaces provide regular-sized or out-sized classroom spaces as needed. In a number of junior-high schools, as many as four or six regular-sized classrooms are clustered in such a way that when their walls are opened a single large space of three thousand to five thousand square feet is created. One of these, in Jefferson County, Colorado, has an experimental, electrically operated wall with a completely retractable baseboard that lifts up into a space behind the chalkboard. The entire wall can then be moved forward or backward over the furniture in its path. When the wall is shared by two adjoining classrooms, one space can be reduced and the other enlarged.

Schools Without Partitions. Some schools are experimenting with the elimination of partitions altogether. Large open spaces of various geometric shapes (spheres, hexagons, squares, and even a volute [6]), each containing the equivalent of three to five conventional classrooms, are to be found in an increasing number of new

---

6. The snail-shaped Valley Winds School in Riverview Gardens (St. Louis County), Missouri, is one of the country's most talked-about schools. It embodies nearly all the ideas associated with the educational reform movement.

schools. The teachers in these spaces usually work as a team, and often the programs are nongraded as well. There is already an impressive literature in support of wall-less classrooms,[7] and the feasibility and desirability of teaching in large open spaces are becoming evident to the profession.

In most of these schools the teachers have unusual opportunities to pool their talents and to work closely together. They can observe and help one another as they teach, and they usually share a team office in which professional planning and conversation are easily carried on. The pupils enjoy a close working association with one another and with their teachers, in an unusually flexible setting.

The question most frequently asked about classrooms without walls is, "But what about the noise?" Oddly enough, noise problems have not proved severe, partly because floor carpeting and other acoustical devices have been provided, and partly because the teachers have learned to coordinate their schedules and isolate such noise-producing activities as singing. Furthermore, acoustical engineers have concluded that the amount of sound interception necessary between groups may be much less than has been assumed. With careful use of sound-absorbing materials and good manipulation of the space itself, it now seems possible to enjoy freedom from distraction in open spaces. In fact, experience suggests that it is better not to use acoustical ceilings with a carpeted floor, lest the room be too quiet. It also suggests that the overall space must be large enough in relation to the pupil population to permit adequate separation between work groups.[8]

Provisions for Individual Learning. For some years now, authorities have advocated that the amount of school time allocated to individual study be increased. Some have suggested 40 percent as a desirable allotment. The architectural implications of this recommendation are almost breathtaking. Should every student have a "home base" in the library or in some other appropriate location? Can a school get along with fewer classrooms and a greater proportion of space devoted to individual studies and projects? Can

7. *Profiles of Significant Schools: Schools Without Walls,* New York: Educational Facilities Laboratories, 1965. Jan Goss, "Teaching in the Big Room," *The National Elementary Principal,* 44 (January 1965), pp. 79–82.
8. Special advantages and the solution of technical problems are discussed in detail in *Schools Without Walls, op. cit.*

more of the pupils' school experience be removed to the home, or to the public library, or to some other location? Some observers answer all these questions in the affirmative.

In colleges and in private boarding schools there is already a trend toward the use of dormitory rooms and other living quarters as adjunct learning spaces. Telephone connections, wireless radio connections, television, and other means of direct contact are made between a central control center and each student location, so that the students can listen to or watch a lesson (which may be computer-assisted) and respond to it. Instruction over closed-circuit television and public educational channels is already an established procedure, and with video-taping it is now possible for almost any program to be presented to a given student or group of students at almost any time. As a result, we can conceive of a school program that extends into dormitories and private homes at all times of the week. How soon this development will affect the typical public school is difficult to predict. The technological revolution is still in its infancy, and school practice in the future is destined to be profoundly affected by mechanical and electronic resources.

In the next chapter we will discuss the ways in which libraries and instructional materials centers promise to provide for individual learning. Much imaginative work has been done in developing study carrels for use by pupils in college and secondary schools and in elementary schools as well. Some of these are little more than knee-spaces, while others are very elaborate units. An extreme, perhaps, was the "studysphere" depicted in a New York World's Fair publication in 1964. Among its features were an antenna, temperature controls, ionized air control, light control, television and film screen, microphone, tape cartridge insert for the recording and playback of taped materials, stereo speakers in chair wings, a light-sensitive writing surface and instant printer, typing keys, and an adjustable seat. Many of these features are already found in carrel models on the market or in experimental use, and it is not unreasonable to expect that schools will some day furnish individual spaces with communication equipment as generously as they now furnish spaces for group instruction.

Schools That Look to the Future. From time to time we have mentioned certain schools that look to the future in significant ways. There are hundreds of schools around the country that deserve special mention, and to single out only a few of them may be unfair. However, to comment on some features of particular interest may give us a better picture of the changing American schoolhouse.

1. Hancock High School, Washington County, Maryland, has a floor plan designed with television in mind. The classrooms are clustered around the four sides of a large television viewing area that has no windows and is therefore free of direct sunlight.

2. Wayland High School, Wayland, Massachusetts, is one of the first schools to be designed with "planned variability." The domed physical-education plant has also attracted wide interest.

3. Granada Community School, Reed Union School District, California, has open-classroom clusters, designed on a 960-square-foot hexagonal module (four in each cluster, plus a central common), that provide team centers for each family of nongraded, multiaged pupils. In future expansion there will be a unique teacher-education center with an instructional materials area, a professional research library, carrels and office space, adult seminar classrooms, and a closed-circuit television studio.

4. John F. Kennedy High School, Plainview–Old Bethpage School District, Long Island, New York, has clusters of standard-sized classrooms arranged so that each room may be used separately or in combinations of two, three, or four for larger-group instruction.

5. Douglas School, Flowing Wells School District, Tucson, Arizona, is a collection of four circular buildings. Each is capable of being divided into six pie-shaped areas, one of which serves as a library-commons area. In the center is a teachers' office area, with each teacher just a few steps away from her own classroom.

6. Bedford Middle School, Mount Kisco, New York, has three academic "houses," each accommodating about 330 pupils, located around a central octagonal arts building. The auditorium can be divided into sections by a soundproof folding partition. Unusual opportunities for individual study are provided in a large open library area and in individual study carrels capable of seating about two-thirds of the pupils in each house.

7. Kennedy Junior High School, Natick, Massachusetts, has double-coiled, sound-insulated, electrically operated partitions that can divide the auditorium into three separate areas seating 100, 250, and 100 pupils, respectively. It is also a three-house school, but all three houses are under one roof. The relatively small library can be expanded into adjoining study halls.

8. Barrington Middle School, Barrington, Illinois, is intended

for grades 6–7–8. It consists of four wings leading out from a large central core with an open learning center (seven thousand square feet) and a multipurpose dining area. Each wing contains 11,750 square feet of carpeted, air-conditioned, unobstructed loft space. It is one of the first schools in the country to be constructed in accordance with the School Construction Systems Development system of modular components, as developed in California with the assistance of Educational Facilities Laboratories.

9. P.S. 45, Brooklyn, New York, is a prize-winning urban school with no windows on the sides facing the streets (to discourage vandals and reduce outside noise) and is built around an inner courtyard. Among its unique features is a new method of serving hot school lunches: a conveyor belt carries prepared frozen food (the freezer holds a two-week supply) which is heated in four large convection ovens.

10. The C. Thurston Chase Learning Center (added in 1965 to the Eaglebrook School), Deerfield, Massachusetts, includes a science building with convertible laboratory-classroom space. There are an exhibition-assembly room, an unusually fine library with an office and a curriculum planning area for the faculty, and a balcony with sound booths for the students and a faculty research area.

11. The James Madison Wood Quadrangle, Stephens College, Columbia, Missouri, is a learning center that makes extensive use of the new communications media. It consists of five buildings linked together by a unified electronics system.

This list could be extended for many pages. Two developments it does not mention are (1) the educational park or plaza and (2) various proposals for building schools in congested urban areas where land is at a premium. The latter topic is skillfully examined in an article by William W. Chase,[9] who describes schools built over land that is being used for other urban purposes (for example, subway yards) or on a joint-occupancy basis with offices or apartments. The educational park is an effort to bring an entire K–12 (or preschool-through-college) school system into a campus-like setting that permits maximum articulation and coordination among units. A well-known example is the Nova complex in Fort Lauderdale, Florida.

---

9. "Schoolhouses for Big Cities," *American Education*, 1 (February 1965), pp. 12–19.

GETTING THE SCHOOLS WE NEED

It would be foolish to assert that good school programs depend on good school buildings. The quality of the people who work in the buildings is the real key to a first-rate program. Many of the most exciting achievements in American education (e.g., the teaching-team project in the Franklin School, Lexington, Massachusetts) took place in inappropriate buildings, and in some excellent buildings only bland, stale, or uninteresting things are happening (as in some of the so-called laboratory schools associated with colleges of education). However, the most propitious conditions exist when both the staff and the setting in which they work are of the highest quality. Unsuitable buildings can and do inhibit the full development of certain organizational and instructional ideas, and staffs that are unable or unwilling to exploit the advantages of a flexible building can thwart the best-laid plans of a community. How, then, can school systems arrange for the best possible combination?

Cyril Sargent has pointed out that the imaginative use of existing spaces, some of which can be modified and modernized at relatively low cost, is an excellent way of introducing and developing new programs, not only as a means of preparing the staff for innovation but as a way of discovering the space relationships that are needed.[10] Every existing school probably has some unused or wasted space, some rooms that could be partitioned, and some permanent walls that could be removed or replaced with folding sections. Often these changes can be made inexpensively and in stages that allow for experimentation along the way. For example, one school decided to remove a nonloadbearing wall between two classrooms in order to create a room for occasional large-group instruction. The wall was torn down by the custodian crew over a Christmas holiday, and the plan was to install a rather expensive sound-proof folding partition the next month. Luckily the partition was not delivered on time, and the teachers improvised by bringing some old rugs out of their attics as temporary sound insulation on the floors. To their surprise the "temporary" arrangement worked out very well, and eventually the order for the folding partition was canceled and wall-to-wall carpeting was installed instead. The teachers continue to work in an open area equivalent to two class-

---

10. Sargent, *op. cit.*, p. 239.

rooms, and their experience has led to the planning of similar open space in a new addition.

Many communities do not have time to improvise and experiment because their new schools must be planned *now*. Moreover, not all the members of their professional staff may be ready to commit themselves to such arrangements as team teaching. What can such a community do?

If neither the school leaders nor a substantial number of the teachers have any interest in departing from conventional patterns, and if there is no active group of citizens ready to do battle, there is little hope that a suitable and flexible school will be built. The community will probably build a conventional school which within ten or fifteen years will be recognized as obsolete. Then the taxpayers will raise the futile cry, "Why didn't somebody warn us?"

But on every staff there are some teachers with an eye on the future and a sense of what is needed. These teachers must make themselves audible to their colleagues and to the citizenry alike. They must argue for an experimental attitude, flexibility, and the opportunity to demonstrate some of the requirements of tomorrow's schools. They must give all possible support and encouragement to the administration by advocating convertible, versatile, malleable, and variable spaces in the design of new buildings.

At worst, the new facilities might go unexploited for a decade or so. But the successors of these venturesome teachers would find that changes and improvements were possible because of good architectural planning, and as a result the building would be put to good use for the next thirty to fifty years. At best the new building might stimulate better practices from the beginning.

It is far better in the long run for a new building to be more modern than its staff than for a new building to suffer from obsolescence when the next generation of teachers is ready to take over. Teachers can and do change over the years, but buildings have a way of being built to last. America cannot afford to invest its precious resources in expensive buildings that are unsuited to the task that lies ahead, and those teachers in America who have the clearest vision of that task must be sure their views are heard.

Suggestions for Class Discussion and Further Investigation

1. There are a number of filmstrips (with accompanying narratives on tapes or records) and sound films designed to stimu-

late thinking about the design and construction of school-houses. Some of these, available from the National Education Association, are "Focus on Change," "Focus on the Individual," and "Planning and Organizing for Teaching." Of particular interest is "To Build a Schoolhouse," a twenty-eight-minute film available from Educational Facilities Laboratories. Ask your instructor to arrange for a showing. Later, discuss with your classmates such questions as (a) Why do schools need so much flexibility? (b) Do such features as air conditioning and floor carpeting make an *educational* difference, or is comfort their only advantage? (c) What would it be like to teach in an open space alongside other teachers? (d) How does the design of a building hinder or assist the educational program?

2. Visit an older school with some of your friends. Try to determine (a) the ways in which the building seems to be dictating or influencing some of the educational practices of the staff and (b) the ways in which the available space might be used more flexibly and imaginatively. Pretend, for example, that you and some other teachers are going to rent the building in order to run an experimental summer school. What would you do to ensure maximum flexibility in your school building?

3. Talk with a superintendent, a school-board member, or some other official in a place where a new school has recently been constructed. Ascertain both from discussion and from your own observations how modern and flexible the new plant is, and then try to discover the reasons for its flexibility. Ask what part the staff played in planning, and find out what the staff's recommendations were. Try to estimate the amount and type of leadership each group exercised (or failed to exercise) during the planning stages. Then discuss the results with your classmates and speculate on what might have been done to improve the situation.

4. Walter Hill, an architect in Cambridge, Massachusetts, has proposed that in the school of the future students will carry about a "mobile desk" the size of a briefcase that will contain both audio and visual systems capable of storing and disseminating information. It will also be capable of reacting to and recording students' responses. By telephone connec-

tion or other means of contact, information will be transferred either to or from this "individual learning center." Discuss with your classmates some of the implications of this idea for independent study within the school, for homework and other out-of-school studies, and for the teacher-pupil relationship.

5. Interview a dozen or more children of a given age. (Each of your classmates might select a different age, so that your aggregate data would present the entire K–12 school population.) Ask the children one question: "What makes a good school?" You will discover that many of their responses have nothing to do with the physical building, that some are partly related to the building, and that some are entirely concerned with the structure. Classify the responses, and then judge some existing schools in accordance with the pupils' criteria.

Suggestions for Further Reading

As we have indicated, Educational Facilities Laboratories has produced the most significant literature in this field in recent years. In addition to the publications cited in footnotes, see: *Design for ETV: Planning for Schools with Television* (1960), *Profiles of Significant Schools: Schools for Team Teaching* (1961), *Profile of a Significant School: Riverview Gardens Elementary Schools* (1964; available from the School Planning Laboratory, University of Tennessee, Knoxville, Tennessee), and *Middle Schools* (1965).

Cyril G. Sargent's chapter, "The Organization of Space," in Judson T. Shaplin and Henry F. Olds, Jr., eds., *Team Teaching*, New York: Harper and Row, 1964, pp. 216–40, and a similar chapter in Medill Bair and Richard G. Woodward, *Team Teaching in Action*, Boston: Houghton Mifflin, 1964, pp. 36–60, are extremely informative, as is Donald P. Mitchell's excellent article, "Housing Cooperative Teaching Programs," *The National Elementary Principal*, 44 (January 1965), pp. 44–52. The Mitchell article also appears in Maurice Hillson and Harvey B. Scribner, eds., *Readings in Collaborative and Team Approaches to Teaching and Learning*, New York: Selected Academic Readings, 1965.

Of considerable interest, too, is Harold B. Gores' chapter, "Schoolhouse in Transition," *The Changing American School,* The Sixty-fifth Yearbook of the National Society for the Study of Education, Part II, Chicago: Univ. of Chicago Press, 1966.

Chapter Eight

The Library-centered School

by SARA JAFFARIAN, Coordinator, Instructional Materials, Lexington (Massachusetts) Public Schools

There can be no excellent school without a library.
                                                    —BENJAMIN LEE SMITH [1]

"Every school needs a library," announced the Joint Library Committee of NESDEC–NESLA [2] on a cold New England day in 1952. More than five hundred administrators, professors, teachers, and librarians had gathered to listen to the report. For two years representatives from thirty-four communities had been seeking answers to such questions as: What does a good school library do for the pupil, the teacher, and the community? What are its needs in personnel, materials, and equipment? How can it secure support? John B. Davis, Jr. (NESDEC executive secretary), said, "The study will serve as a criterion for judging standards of school libraries, and as an instrument for the heightening of interest in the school library."

The published report became an NESDEC "best seller," with international sales. At last a significant breakthrough had been made, for now librarians, teachers, administrators, and laymen were talking with one another about the library's involvement in promoting good quality education. After that day in 1952, such local, regional, and national conferences and jointly issued publications became increasingly common.

Today there seems to be little question about the need for a library within the school. In both popular and professional writ-

---

1. While Dr. Smith was superintendent of the Greensboro, North Carolina, public schools, Sara Jaffarian served as Director of Libraries in the Greensboro school system. Dr. Smith had long been a champion of school libraries and had insisted that his own school libraries meet national standards. The statement quoted here appeared as the opening sentence of "Is Your Child a Victim of the 'Library Gap'?" *This Week* magazine (April 16, 1961).
2. *Every School Needs a Library*, Cambridge, Mass.: New England School Development Council–New England School Library Association, 1952. NESDEC is a voluntary association of school systems, with offices located at Harvard University.

ing, evidence and argument are mustered in favor of the library as a valuable and necessary resource. Nearly every discussion of school curriculum and scheduling stresses the importance of library-based independent and group study. Both the National Education Association and the American Library Association (ALA) urge that a library—or, as it is variously called today, an instructional materials center, a resource center, and a learning laboratory—be provided in every school. Such a library must be stocked with a wide range of educational materials including books, magazines, films, phonograph records, tapes, pictures, pamphlets, and transparencies all centrally organized for efficient distribution. But what of the years before 1952?

HISTORICAL PERSPECTIVE

Early Development. The school library had its beginnings in 1835, but almost a century passed before it was recognized as a necessary part of the school, and then almost exclusively at the secondary level. Even though several states had passed laws for tax levies to support school libraries as early as 1835, the dominant pattern of library service from 1876 to 1920 was that of cooperation between the school and the public library. Urban communities with public libraries lent collections to the classroom teacher for reference or collateral reading.

During the 1920's the number of high-school libraries grew at a rapid rate. The main impetus was provided by the adoption in 1920 of minimum quantitative standards by the North Central Association of Colleges and Secondary Schools; these standards were based on recommendations developed by joint library and education study committees. Elementary-school libraries lagged, despite the publication of another set of standards in 1925. The 1933 NEA *Yearbook* noted that the public library still provided extensive service to schools and that elementary schools still depended almost exclusively on the public library for books through a school-loan deposit collection arrangement, bookmobile stops at the school, and branch libraries located within the school. This pattern gradually disappeared in the 1950's as public libraries began to rechannel their limited funds into more traditional services. School authorities, left without books, were forced to recognize the need for having library materials readily and permanently available within the school itself.

Now, for the first time in history, federal legislation has earmarked financial grants specifically for the development of school libraries. The 1958 National Defense Education Act extended the use of audio-visual materials and equipment in the schools. The Elementary and Secondary Act of 1965 promises to have a similar effect on the development of central school libraries. Fortunately, the legislators who drafted this act took into account the best of current thinking on the place of the school library in education. During the next five years millions of children will for the first time have access to a substantial supply of library books and supplementary instructional materials.

Evolvement of the Instructional Materials Concept. The publication of standards and the requirements of accrediting associations have had a marked influence on the growth and development of school libraries. A section on the school library in the "evaluative criteria" published in 1940 by the Cooperative Study of Secondary School Standards reinforced and expanded the emerging philosophy that the effective high-school library no longer could be merely a collection of books but must be a center for the educational life of the school. The 1950 edition of the criteria further stressed the need for qualified library staff members and recommended that audio-visual materials be made available for use in the educational program, either through the library or through a separate department. The most recent (1960) criteria recommend that the school provide an "instructional materials center." A 1956 statement by the American Association of School Librarians (AASL)—a division of the ALA and the NEA—had prepared the way for this newer philosophy.

The statements of the AASL and the "evaluative criteria" were based on secondary education practices of the 1950's which emphasized intellectual excellence and individual differences. Both statements recommended that the instructional materials center staff perform several functions: (1) provide a rich variety of materials, including books and other printed materials, recordings, still and motion pictures, filmstrips and other audio-visual materials and resources, for use by teachers and students as individuals and in groups; (2) offer leadership in developing techniques for the use of various materials by the teachers and students; (3) make available facilities, services, and equipment necessary for the selection, organization, and use of instructional materials; and (4) furnish facilities for and assistance in the production of instructional materials and displays. The primary responsibility for administering such a center could be either the librarian's alone or shared by him with the audio-visual materials staff.

A 1958 statement prepared by the Joint Committee of the AASL, the Association of College and Research Libraries (ACRL), and the Division of Audio-Visual Instruction (DAVI) of the NEA indicated concern lest some instructional materials and services be given preference over others. This joint statement stressed that the distinctive characteristics of each type of material or medium— whether it be educational television, specialized training devices, projections, books, films, recordings, field trips, or classroom discussion—should be recognized for their unique contribution in achieving the teaching-learning objective. Instructional materials specialists "need to have a working knowledge of the entire range of media, of the potential contributions each can make to learning and the most effective methods of use in order to assist teachers to locate, evaluate, select, produce, and use instructional materials to best advantage." [3] The statement also noted that all three associations were vitally concerned with the study, development, and application of all types of instructional materials, and that all three had important responsibilities for the recruitment, professional education, and certification of school, college, and university staff members who would serve as specialists.

PHILOSOPHY OF THE 1960'S

The *Standards for School Library Programs,* published early in 1960 by the ALA after an intensive five-year study, sets forth the goals and standards for a program of library service considered essential to the modern curriculum. Representatives of eighteen educational associations and of the General Federation of Women's Clubs joined with a committee of the AASL to formulate the standards after analyzing the school library program in its relationship to the changing curriculum and to the goals of elementary and secondary education. The study was based on answers to questionnaires sent to school systems throughout the country which were considered to have outstanding school library programs. At two

---

3. American Association of School Librarians, *Standards for School Library Programs,* Chicago: American Library Association, 1960, pp. 59–61.

national library conferences, study groups analyzed the results and offered recommendations on personnel, materials, and equipment. Among the matters discussed in the ALA publication are the school library as an educational force, the planning and implementation of school library programs, and quantitative and qualitative measures of resources for teaching and learning.

Briefly, the standards recommend a basic book collection of six thousand to ten thousand volumes for a school with 200 to 999 students, and at least ten books per student for larger schools. Annual expenditures for books, allocated regularly from the school budget, should be from four to six dollars per student, with additional amounts for magazines and other materials. Audio-visual material expenditures of 1 percent of the instructional materials budget were recommended. To conduct an adequate program of services, one trained librarian (with certification in education and library science) for each three hundred students or major fraction thereof was advocated. Attractive, functional quarters designed to meet the needs of the program and to accommodate approximately 10 percent of the student body at one time were among the other recommendations.

Implementation of the Standards. The School Library Development Project (SLDP), which operated from February 1961 to July 1962, was established with a grant from the Council on Library Resources and was based at the ALA headquarters in Chicago. By furnishing consultant service to state and local groups and by distributing publications developed through further studies, this project greatly helped to implement the 1960 standards set by AASL and educational groups. Regional and state workshops, under the guidance of the SLDP staff, worked for local adoption of the national standards.

The Knapp Foundation in New York City made a grant of $1,130,000 to ALA in 1962 to "help implement library standards in United States schools." A National Library Week article, "Is Your Child a Victim of the 'Library Gap'?" [4] had come to the Foundation's attention. Five elementary and three secondary schools across the country were given supplementary funds to bring their services in materials, personnel, and facilities in line with ALA standards; these schools are serving as demonstration centers for a five-year

---

4. *This Week* magazine (April 16, 1961).

period.[5] Each center is linked by contract to a neighboring teacher-training institution which provides a field worker to help co-ordinate the library service program with its student teacher-training program. The project also provides funds for visitation teams of librarians, educators, and citizens. The influence of this program has been far reaching.

The Encyclopaedia Britannica School Library Awards, presented annually since 1963 to school systems doing an outstanding job of improving their elementary school libraries, have also created wide-spread interest. The purpose of these awards is to "help promote implementation of the national school library standards and to in-crease interest in the development of elementary school librar-ies." [6] An AASL committee screens applications and makes recom-mendations for recipients of the cash awards that are presented to the local school system during National Library Week.

The Role of the Librarian. Until 1930 the two main functions of the high-school librarian were to buy books and reference materials and to teach pupils how to use the library. Library instruction has gradually become integrated with the reference and research projects of the classroom, and the isolated lesson in library science has dis-appeared.

In addition to instruction in the use of the library, today's librar-ian (1) is familiar with the reading interests and abilities of the students in the school so that he can help foster independent read-ing programs, (2) is responsible for helping pupils and teachers use those materials best suited to solving the problem at hand, (3) helps with curriculum development, (4) solicits and accepts requests for books and materials to be acquired, (5) discusses with class groups specific materials related to courses of study, (6) meets with department heads and team groups to discuss their needs, and (7) provides books and materials of professional interest to the faculty.

5. The Demonstration Project schools are: Central Park Road Elementary School, Plainview, New York; Marcus Whitman Elementary School, Richland, Washington; Allisonville School, Marion County, Indiana; Mount Royal School, Baltimore, Maryland; and Casis Elementary School, Austin, Texas. Secondary schools include: Oak Park and River Forest High School, Illinois; Roosevelt High School, Portland, Oregon; and Farrer Junior High School, Provo, Utah.
6. Data on expenditures, personnel, collections, and quarters of the 159 school system applications are appraised in an effort to identify patterns of develop-ment and highlight effective practices in elementary school library services in Mary V. Gaver, *Patterns of Development in Elementary School Libraries Today,* 2nd ed., Chicago: Encyclopaedia Britannica, 1965.

At a recent library conference a school principal said, "One of the librarian's important and rewarding duties is teaching teachers how to become better teachers through using the library." The librarian does this by helping them learn how to relate their teaching to library services and materials. Whatever the level—preschool, elementary, junior high, or senior high—the librarian's responsibility is basically the same.

The circulation of materials to classrooms is still another important phase of the librarian's responsibility. He assists teachers in the selection of various types of materials for short- or long-term classroom loans. The teacher needs supplementary teaching resources close at hand during particular study units. If audio-visual equipment such as viewers and projectors is housed in the central library it too may be borrowed along with the materials of instruction. The new campus-style high schools use special subject collections in "satellite" libraries as a means of getting materials closer to students and teachers. Flexibility in location, distribution, and loan patterns of the materials center are necessary if it is to fulfill its purpose.

Central Supervision for Program Coordination and Development. Another recent development in school library service has been an increase in the number of administrative positions created for the system-wide coordination and promotion of such programs. In 1950 there were fewer than two hundred librarians in such positions, but by 1965 the number had more than doubled. A librarian serving in this capacity for a school system is known variously as a consultant, supervisor, coordinator, or director of library or instructional materials services. His major responsibility is to formulate goals and policies for such system-wide services as (1) the development of criteria for selecting materials; (2) the provision of inservice training of librarians and teachers; (3) the administration of library budgets; (4) the centralized ordering, cataloging, and processing of materials for all the schools; (5) the planning of library quarters; (6) the establishment of a research and development library for teachers; (7) the preparation of reports and statistics for the use of local administrators who must interpret the library program to the community; (8) the preparation of annual budget requests for the various schools; (9) the preparation of reports on the local program as required by state and federal agencies; (10) the evaluation of the quality of the library program in each of the schools, with recommendations for long-range development; and (11) the advancement of the philosophy underlying the community's educational program.

In an effort to improve the use of all types of instructional materials, system-wide audio-visual and library supervisory services are being consolidated into one department. With the school library as an instructional materials center, teachers and pupils can satisfy their needs for all types of learning material more easily and efficiently. The supervisor in charge of such a program of services must be trained in all phases of instructional materials. In the case of large school systems, specialists in the various media may be part of the central staff.

Although national standards recommend one library supervisor for any school system of five or more schools, the U.S. Office of Education (USOE) 1960 surveys indicated that no more than 4 percent of all school systems in the country had such positions; only 640 public school districts had a supervisor of library services. In 1965 the AASL School Library Supervisors Section reported a figure closer to 10 percent. Most large cities and a growing number of suburban communities already are providing such supervisory services.

IMPACT OF LEGISLATION

Shocking substandard conditions in school libraries came to light in studies undertaken in the 1960's by the USOE and several state education departments. According to the U.S. Commissioner of Education, who referred to the low status of libraries as a "national disgrace," over ten million American students attend schools without any libraries, and 60 percent of the elementary schools have no central libraries. Recent state and federal legislation has attempted to remedy the situation.

Amendments to the National Defense Education Act of 1964 expanded the 1958 act (which had concentrated on mathematics, science, and foreign languages) to include financial assistance for materials and equipment to strengthen instruction in history, civics, geography, English, and reading. For each year from 1964 to 1967 the federal government authorized grants of over $32 million to institutions of higher education for the training of teachers and supervisors in these subject fields and for the training of educational media specialists and librarians. Interest was so high during the first year that thousands of qualified applicants could not be accommodated. The program has helped alleviate the shortage of trained personnel.

The most promising step in school library development is the 1965 Elementary and Secondary Education Act, Title II of which focuses on improving school libraries. The act provided an outright grant of $100 million for fiscal 1966, allocated to the states on the basis of enrollment. This grant was for the purchase of classroom texts, library books, musical scores, maps, video tapes, photographs, and other printed and audio-visual materials. Each state develops its own plans for strengthening the school instructional materials program. Local school systems, in applying to state departments of education for funds, must indicate the quantity and quality of available resources and describe the programs they are planning to undertake.

Title III of the ESEA is designed to strengthen leadership in state departments of education. Fourteen states have been able to initiate school library consultant services by adding a school library supervisor to their staffs, and other states have been able to enlarge staffs for greater field service. The function of the state school library consultant is to advise public school personnel who are initiating school library programs or expanding existing programs. Field visits, conferences, correspondence, and publications are some of the means used. Since the state education agencies are responsible for administering the ESEA, those sections concerned with the school library are the responsibility, by and large, of the state school library consultant. This consultant has a great deal of influence on how the federal funds are spent in school districts, because all proposals for use of the funds must first be approved by the state education agency. Title I of the act provides additional funds to the local agencies for strengthening educational programs for children of low-income families; some of these funds will certainly be spent on materials for school libraries.

Still another federal act, the 1965 Higher Education Bill, provides assistance for training school librarians. Recent statistics show the ratio of qualified librarians to pupils in public schools is one to 1,254; yet national standards call for one librarian for every three hundred pupils. USOE figures from a sample study updated to 1963–64 show that there should be 112,000 school librarians (each with fifteen hours or more of library training) to meet

ALA standards; yet only 25,000 are so qualified. In 1966, 84 percent of the elementary schools in the nation lacked trained librarians on their staffs, even though there was a demand for service at this age level. Capable classroom teachers are being encouraged to take training in library work at state universities, colleges, and schools of education. These institutions are expanding their programs to help meet the requirements of state teacher-librarian certification laws (normally twelve to twenty-four semester hours). However, an excellent program requires a library staff trained in depth, both in academic subjects and in library science (i.e., staff members should have a master's degree in library science from an ALA-accredited school).

NEW MATERIALS

Books, Paperbacks, Films, and Computers. The volume of publications intended for readers of elementary and secondary school age promises to keep pace with increasing enrollments. Statistics from the Book Manufacturers Institute show that sales of juvenile books costing over one dollar doubled from 1954 to 1965. The number of new books published for juveniles rose from 410 in 1920 to more than 2,600 in 1965. The juvenile category is steadily increasing in the percentage of total book production. Authors, illustrators, editors, and specialists are combining their talents and efforts to produce attractive books of high quality to enrich formal class work at all levels. Librarians acquaint publishers with the demands and needs of the classroom to assure the availability of the best books possible, not only to meet reference and curriculum enrichment needs, but also to aid in the personal reading enrichment of young people.

In October 1965 the First National Conference on Paperbacks in Education, sponsored by Teachers College of Columbia University and attended by nearly seven hundred educators, explored the use of paperbacks in the schools. Of the thirty-five thousand paperbacks in print at that time, at least five thousand could be considered appropriate for use in the schools. Quality paperbacks are on the increase, and many schools are using them as supplements to texts. School libraries are also adding paperback collections to meet rising demands.

Another promising educational device is the 8-mm film, which has now made motion pictures one of the simplest of all pictorial media to use. The cost of production is relatively low, and students and teachers can make their own films with nearly automatic cameras; sound can be recorded on a magnetic strip added to the film. Teachers College of Columbia University is presently under contract to the USOE to produce a film and a manual on the uses of 8-mm film in education. More than 1,600 cartridges of commercially produced silent film loops were available in 1965. A similar boom is occurring in the commercial production of 16-mm films, filmstrips, recordings, and several other types of instructional materials.

The "knowledge explosion" of recent years has created concern about how the flood of new material can be organized for ready access and quick retrieval. Many colleges and universities and large community libraries have turned to some type of computerized system. Several conferences are held each year to study information storage and retrieval. At a conference held at the Massachusetts Institute of Technology late in 1965, the prediction was made that students and scholars will soon be using libraries "not only to locate books and documents in the library, but also to gain access to the university's total information resources, through touch-tone telephones, teletypewriter keyboards, television-like displays, and quickly made copies. . . . The information traffic will be controlled by means of a time-shared computer utility on the campus in much the same way that today's verbal communications are handled by the campus telephone exchange." [7] Developments of this sort will require that secondary-school students be trained to use college libraries in the years ahead.

FACILITIES FOR THE SCHOOL LIBRARY

The school library, if it is to provide proper service to the educational community, must be a spacious and well-planned component of the school building. It must be suitable in size and location. It must be functional, attractive, and comfortable. A well-designed library makes it possible for pupils to read or work individually or in groups. It must have stack areas for books, workrooms for librarians and audio-visual specialists, space for the use of audio-visual materials and adequate and suitable storage spaces. It should

---

7. Carl F. J. Overhage, ed., *Intrex: The Report of a Planning Conference on Information Transfer Experiments,* Cambridge, Mass.: MIT Press, 1965.

have study carrels [8] and other individual working areas. It may also include space to be used in the future for electronic equipment linking the center to distant information centers and libraries. Ideally it should also include space reserved for the use of teachers and other professionals as they go about their curriculum planning and study.

Until recently, most of the literature on school libraries focused on secondary schools and colleges. It is not necessary to repeat here what has been so well stated about secondary-school libraries.[9] However, it may be of interest to examine an elementary-school library that was planned as an instructional materials center.

A CASE STUDY

In 1963, Superintendent Benjamin C. Willis of the Chicago public schools became director of a comprehensive study of education problems in Massachusetts. The summary report of the Willis Commission [10] stressed the importance of having in every school library resources that would meet ALA standards. In 1965, Lexington was the only public school system in Massachusetts with a library program that in general met the Willis recommendations. It fell short, however, of national standards for staff, space, and materials. Lexington had made rapid strides since 1961 in developing a total library program for grades 1–12. By placing second in the 1964 Encyclopaedia Britannica Library Awards program, Lexington won national recognition for its school system. The attendant publicity further awakened the community and the school staff to the need for greater financial support of school library services. The school committee (the board of education) and the school administration are publicly committed to developing a strong instructional materials service program.

In 1965, in only one of the nine elementary schools in Lexing-

---

8. A discussion of various types of carrels and their use appears in Ralph E. Ellsworth and Hobart D. Wagener, *The School Library: Facilities for Independent Study in the Secondary School,* New York: Educational Facilities Laboratories, 1963, pp. 56–67.
9. *Ibid.* A "gallery of prototype architectural designs" is discussed on pages 97–136, and the "bibliography" is given on pages 137–39.
10. Benjamin C. Willis, *Quality Education for Massachusetts: An Investment in the People of the Commonwealth,* Summary Report of the Special Commission Relative to Improving and Extending Educational Facilities in the Commonwealth, Boston: The Commonwealth of Massachusetts, December 1965.

ton had a library room been provided for in the original design of the building. Two of these schools had been built as recently as 1956. An elementary school designed expressly for team teaching, which opened in 1961, did have about eighteen hundred square feet for use as a "resource center," but the equipment installed in the center was limited to book and magazine shelving and to traditional library furniture. Darkroom facilities and storage space for audio-visual materials were available elsewhere in the building. These areas soon proved inadequate for the teaching-learning needs of six hundred pupils. The school now has more than 5,000 books, 700 filmstrips, 300 phonorecordings, 25 periodical subscriptions, and an extensive file of pamphlets. Lexington has learned that a full-time librarian is a necessity too if a school with a wealth of centrally organized materials is to be properly served. Now the planning of new elementary schools has taken on new meaning in terms of staff and space.

Two elementary schools of identical construction were voted by Lexington, one slated to open in 1966, the other in 1967. Each will house six hundred pupils, twenty-four classroom teachers, various subject specialists, and a librarian trained as an instructional materials specialist.

Superintendent of Schools Rudolph J. Fobert recently told a parent-teacher group:

> I believe that a school building should facilitate the educational program. The educational program should be developed first and then a building designed to house it. . . .
> At the heart of the building will be the instructional materials or resource center. In this center all recorded data will be housed. This includes books, tapes, records, films, and program-learning machines. Pupils will learn to extract information for independent research, for pleasure, and for group projects; pupils will use machines to improve or enrich skills in the tool subjects.
> A staff workshop will be adjacent to the center so that teachers may have the opportunity to work together to develop the best possible materials for learning. . . .
> In making the resources center the heart of the school, and building the entire school around it, we hope to re-affirm the concept that our primary role is intellectual. Youngsters will be thus encouraged to utilize man's recorded knowledge to achieve a rich and purposeful life.

Early specifications for the proposed schools incorporated the recommendations of a committee of Lexington administrators and staff specialists and those of the present author. As director of school library services for the Greensboro, North Carolina, schools from 1953 to 1960, and for the Seattle, Washington, public schools from 1960 to 1961, I had set up school libraries as instructional materials centers in both communities.

One of the first steps was to list the services that were to be provided by the instructional materials center. I was assigned responsibility to work with the architect as consultant to translate services into areas that would support a functional, efficient, and adequate program. Details of the instructional materials complex were plotted in cognizance of the purpose of the center in relation to the whole school program.

General Plan of the School. A rectangular school plan was chosen for its flexibility in program planning. It contains large- and small-group instruction spaces, folding partitions between classrooms, a gymnasium, a large-group instruction area that serves also as a dining area, an enclosed court for specialized activities, administration offices, and the instructional materials complex.

This last-named area is the "heart" of the school. It is enclosed on two sides by corridors. The main reading room will have an elevated ceiling with clerestory windows. It is easily accessible to all pupils and staff. It can be used during nonschool hours without opening other parts of the school.

Each classroom is equipped with a ceiling-hung screen for viewing and modular shelf and tackboard units to house materials circulated on temporary loan from the central library. The liberal provision of electrical outlets makes possible the use of electronic equipment borrowed from the center. Although closed-circuit television has not yet been provided, there are conduits ready for that purpose. A storage closet adjacent to the large-group instruction area can be used as a television studio.

Facilities in the Instructional Materials Center. The instructional materials center, which is shown in detail in the diagram on page 168, includes a main reading room housing materials for consultation, circulation, and reference, together with space for related activities. A circulation area between the main entrance and the teachers' work area provides a charging desk where records of transactions may be kept by the clerical aide or other assistant. The card catalog of holdings and some reference books are located in this general area. The librarian's desk is situated nearby so that

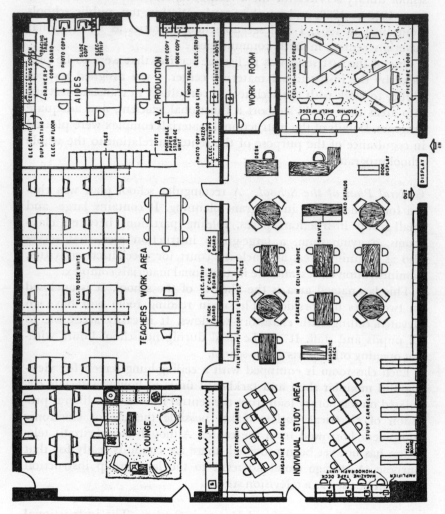

LARGE GROUP INSTRUCTION ROOM

INSTRUCTIONAL MATERIALS CENTER
600 PUPIL ELEMENTARY SCHOOL ~ LEXINGTON, MASS.
SARA JAFFARIAN, CONSULTANT
CRIMP BROWN & FISHER, ARCHITECTS

pupils can turn to him for help as they use the catalogs, bibliographies, and reference tools.

The workroom-office combination has glass partitions that allow for supervision of the larger library spaces. It also includes areas for storing special supplies, preparing new acquisitions, and filing back issues of periodicals.

The teaching materials production area is adjacent to the teachers' permanent stations and the main reading room. This arrangement provides ready accessibility to new source materials as they are being developed. Both teachers and clerical aides who are stationed here will be close to the copying and original production equipment and tools as they assist teachers in the preparation of supplementary teaching materials. One of these aides will be specially trained in the use of the audio-visual equipment and will be under the general supervision of the librarian. Storage cabinets above and below the counters on three sides of the room hold equipment and materials. Counter tops are planned to hold equipment readily available for such procedures as photocopy, diazo, colorlith, book copy, dry copy, slide copy, duplicating, and tracing. A peg-and-tackboard surface and an electrical outlet strip between the counter and the upper cabinets allow for further flexibility of storage and use. There are a movable storage unit for poster paper, vertical files for student records, and a tote-tray unit where teachers may store unfinished materials. A ceiling-hung screen in this work area allows for the quick preview of projected materials.

Records and tapes will be reproduced in the high school, where a sound-proof room is provided adjacent to a language laboratory. This plan makes it possible for several copies of a tape to be reproduced simultaneously. Single tape duplicates can be made at independent, electronically equipped study carrels in the main room of the library.

Facilities for Readers. National standards call for a library seating capacity of at least 10 percent of the school enrollment. Some authorities claim that if the American public is serious in its desire for academic excellence the public must be prepared to pay for a school library that can seat 30 percent of the school's enrollment at one time. This would require seating space for 180 in a 600 enrollment. The Lexington quarters seat twenty-two in a primary-level area (more youngsters could sit on the carpeted floor or on stools), thirty-six in the main reading room at tables, and twenty at individual study carrels. With the large-group instruction room adjacent to the center, and with conference rooms across the corridors, the seating capacity for users of library materials can be increased substantially. The main reading room contains approximately 2,600 square feet, including approximately 150 square feet of floor space for the workroom-office area. The ALA recommendation of twenty-five square feet of floor space per reader was used as a criterion.

The book capacity of the library is 12,000 volumes, with about 3,500 of these on the "easy" or story-book level for primary children. These are shelved in an alcove which has been planned especially for the primary children and is adjacent to the librarian's workroom-office. A sloping top shelf assists young readers in holding large picture books. Another ceiling-hung screen here is used to show the many fine picture-book filmstrips produced by the iconographic process, as well as for viewing other projected materials. The carpeted floor adds to the atmosphere and helps reduce noise; little children like to share their books, and "story hours" are pleasurable group activities.

The ceiling and floor of the main room are acoustically treated, and speakers are hidden in the ceiling. Rectangular tables 36 inches by 60 inches or round ones 48 inches in diameter enable readers to spread out their materials. Chairs and tables are of varying heights (15 to 17 inches for chairs, and 25 to 27 inches for tables) to accommodate children of different sizes.

Other pieces of equipment include display racks for at least twenty-five magazines and for local, regional, and national newspapers; paperback shelving; a new-book display stand; vertical file drawers to house collections of pamphlets and mounted pictures; and cabinets for storing tapes, records, films, filmstrips, and transparencies. There is space available for additional storage units as the need arises. Shelving on the wall next to the teachers' work area will be used for a collection of professional books and magazines for teacher use.

To facilitate independent study there are eleven electronic study carrels permanently equipped with magazine tape decks. Using headphones, students may listen to taped lessons. A dial system can be added to these carrels for the receipt of other sight and sound teaching aids from a central electronic station should one be developed in the school system in the future. Another carrel has a permanent turntable for phonograph recordings. Both individual and group listening are possible with this unit. The other eight carrels are electrically equipped as independent study stations. They will allow the use of portable sound and viewing devices such as filmstrip viewers, teaching machines, radios, 8-inch television receivers, 8-mm cartridge film loops, slide viewers, and portable microfilm readers, as the work of the instructional materials center proceeds. A student may also use books and printed materials at these carrels if he wishes. The printed page will still be at center stage for some years to come, and adequate facilities for housing a collection of high-quality books have been provided.

In the teachers' work area, library personnel and teachers will work together to discuss instructional materials. Teachers, working with the librarian, will plan a list of relevant materials, books, and nonprinted items for temporary use in the classroom. The teacher may examine a collection of project materials assembled by the library staff on a mobile book truck, add to or subtract from the items, and then borrow the truckload for a classroom group. Library-faculty committees may use the area for discussing desired acquisitions in special subject areas, establishing policies for binding or clipping periodicals, and producing materials pertinent to classroom efforts. The librarians advise the teachers on what materials are available for class use, small-group study, and individual work. In short, the area provides a convenient space in which teachers and the library staff can work cooperatively to make the fullest possible use of the whole instructional materials center.

Efficient and flexible physical quarters that will easily lend themselves to a program of educational excellence were always foremost in the minds of the planners. Services may outgrow physical quarters, but the planners hope that the facility will accommodate and encourage experimentation in learning both with present materials and with those yet to be developed.

Marshall McLuhan has said, "Education is ideally civil defense against media fall-out. Yet Western man has had, so far, no education or equipment for meeting any of the new media on their own terms." [11] The Lexington public schools, in their instructional

---

11. *Understanding Media,* New York: McGraw-Hill, 1964, p. 195.

materials centers, are doing their small part in preparing the student for the new media.

Suggestions for Class Discussion and Further Investigation

1. Were there libraries in the elementary and secondary schools that you attended? What types of services were available? Compare these with the types of services described in this chapter.
2. Have a class member report on the 1960 ALA *Standards for School Library Programs*. Invite a local school librarian or the state school library consultant to discuss the standards with you in detail. Discuss methods of implementing them in specific school systems with which you are familiar.
3. A 16-mm sound color film, "And Something More," has been produced by the Knapp School Libraries Project (Chicago, Illinois). Free loan or rental copies are available through state library agencies, regional film libraries, universities, and similar outlets. The film shows the impact of a good school library on the instructional program, and the producers furnish some excellent guidelines for using the film as a basis for discussion and evaluation. Plan a class meeting devoted to a showing of the film and a follow-up discussion.
4. As a teacher, how would you promote independent study by the use of the school library center facilities described in this chapter?
5. Assuming that the school in which you would begin to teach has no professional library for staff members, what types of materials and what books and periodicals would you recommend for purchase?
6. Arrange a panel discussion on the topic "teacher and librarian work together." Discuss specific ways of enriching various subject areas such as science, social studies, language arts, or foreign languages.
7. Increased use of audio-visual techniques is particularly evident in some of the team-teaching projects. In the June 1960 issue of *Grade Teacher* there is an article by Bryce Perkins and his colleagues in the Norwalk Plan (Connecticut), "Team Work Produces Audio-Visual Techniques." Discuss the implications of this article for the teacher and librarian.

Suggestions for Further Reading

As a teacher, you will want to keep abreast of new books that will enrich your classroom instruction. Metropolitan newspapers have book review sections, but a more appropriate source is the book review section of professional magazines. Some examples are: *Elementary English, English Journal, Childhood Education,* and the *NEA Journal.* Publications devoted exclusively to reviewing books for the use of librarians are: the *School Library Journal* (a second section to *Library Journal* and also issued as a separate publication), which reviews books by subject and broad age-level groupings; the *Book Review Digest,* for adult books; the *Bulletin of the Children's Book Center,* a monthly publication of the Laboratory School of the University of Chicago; and the *Horn Book,* a magazine that discusses good literature for children and reviews titles of quality.

Discussions of school library service and special bibliographies of books and nonprinted materials of value to the classroom teacher may be found in the professional journals of librarianship. Three of these are *School Libraries,* the official quarterly of the American Association of School Librarians, and the annual February issue of the *ALA Bulletin* and the November issue of the *Instructor* magazine, both of which are devoted to school libraries.

The U.S. Office of Education sponsored a conference in 1962 to explore new requirements in the professional education of school librarians and teachers "for organizing and using the school library as a materials center to serve modern instructional programs." Its proceedings were published by the U.S. Department of Health, Education and Welfare under the title, *The School Library as a Materials Center: Educational Needs of Librarians and Teachers in Its Administration and Use,"* Mary Helen Mahar, ed.

The January 1966 *Bulletin of the National Association of Secondary School Principals* is entirely devoted to papers submitted by administrators and librarians on the role of the modern school library.

Prospective teachers should familiarize themselves with the work of Bernard Berelson, Edward T. Hall, Paul F. Lazarsfeld, Marshall McLuhan, Ithiel de Sola Pool, and Wilbur Schramm, authorities on the newer media. Two good textbooks for teachers that offer many practical points on the use of audio-visual materials in the classroom are Edgar Dale, *Audio-Visual Methods in Teaching,* 3rd rev. ed. (New York: Holt, Rinehart and Winston, 1965), and Louis Shores, *Instructional Materials: An Introduction for Teachers* (New York: Ronald Press, 1960).

Afterword

The new schools in Lexington are not typical of American elementary schools, nor are some of the exciting secondary schools to which we called attention earlier. However, they help us appreciate what can be done when good planning and a keen sense of the professional mission are injected into the local decision-making process. Obviously, the boys and girls who attend such schools and the adults who work in them are likely to have a profitable, productive, and satisfying experience. Should we not be making such experiences available to *everyone* in American schools?

Questions will of course be raised about the nation's economic capability to carry out such a task, and even about the capability of teachers, administrators, and others to define and achieve their mission with the necessary insight and skill. Not all superintendents see the importance of the things to which Lexington's superintendent dedicated his leadership. Not all librarians see their role in the broad terms outlined in the last chapter. Worse, not enough teachers seem really to care whether or not their resources include the kinds of facilities examined in the last two chapters. It may be that they *do* care, but they raise their voices all too seldom in the cause of better schools.

Throughout this book we have taken note of many exciting ideas that have been introduced into the profession of teaching. Though at times the author's enthusiasms and revolutionary biases may have created an unbalanced or unrealistic view of what is actually happening, or of the forces that seem to resist or militate against progress, it is hoped that the essential flavor of the emerging American school has been accurately caught in these pages. It is hoped, too, that the reader has not lost his essentially optimistic view of a career in education. The book was certainly not intended to dampen in any way the view that teaching is a wonderful and rewarding career. For such, indeed, it is!

The three passwords to this book that we mentioned in the opening chapter were excellence, flexibility, and efficiency. We hope that the meaning and the relevance of these words have become increasingly clear and that the reader has a heightened awareness of the prime importance of a pedagogical orientation, the need for flexibility and variety in pupil groupings, the philosophical and operational virtues of nongraded structure, and the validity of various other trends in the shape and the internal life of the schoolhouse. We hope he agrees that a profession embracing these elements is one worth striving for.

Most of all, we hope he comes away from this book with a feeling of resolve—resolve to stand up for educational reform, to achieve a high professional standard of performance, to make his voice heard. For ultimately the teacher holds within himself the power either to fulfill the American dream of excellence through education or to let his destiny pass him by. An aggressive and courageous willingness to support deserving ideas, and an eagerness to conceive and develop the better ideas that must soon replace them, should be among the qualities for which the teachers of America are known.

Index